Steelhead River Journal

S NORTH UMPQUA

NORTH UMPQUA

by John Shewey

A Frank Amato

PORTLAND

About the Author

John Shewey is a freelance writer and author residing in Bend, Oregon. His articles have appeared in most of the fly angling periodicals and his books include *Northwest Fly Fishing: Trout & Beyond*, *Mastering the Spring Creeks*, and *Alpine Angler*. John fly fishes extensively throughout the Northwest, but summer and fall typically find him chasing steelhead in Oregon, especially on the North Umpqua and Deschutes Rivers. John frequently presents slide shows to angling clubs, with subjects ranging from steelhead to alpine lakes.

Acknowledgements

Joe Howell, owner of the Blue Heron Fly Shop, was a great help in sorting out this project. Thanks Joe, for sharing your insights and your stories. Thanks also to Frank Moore, Mark Powell, Jeff Dose (USDA Forest Service), Dave Loomis (ODFW) and Jim Van Loan (Oregon Fish & Wildlife Commission) for their willingness to discuss some controversial issues involving the North Umpqua. Finally, a special thanks to my fishing partner Forrest Maxwell, who had to fish and fish and fish, all in the name of photography and in pursuit of our favorite game, wild steelhead.

John Shewey
Bend, Oregon

Subscription Information

One year (four issues) $35.00, Two years (eight issues) $65.00. Single copy price $15.95. (Foreign orders add $5.00 per year.) Send check or credit card information to: **Frank Amato Publications, Inc.**, P.O. Box 82112, Portland, Oregon 97282 or call 800-541-9498, Monday through Friday, 9am to 5pm, Pacific Standard Time.

Publisher:
Frank W. Amato

Editor:
Nick Amato

Graphic Production:
Tony Amato

About the Cover: Forrest Maxwell fishes through a run below Steamboat during March. John Shewey photo

All photographs taken by the author unless otherwise noted.
Frontispiece photograph: Richard T. Grost
Title page photograph: Don Roberts
Steelhead River Journal is published four times per year; $15.95 per copy; $35.00 for one year; $65.00 for two years. Foreign orders please add $5.00 per year. Published by Frank Amato Publications, Inc. P.O. Box 82112, Portland, Oregon 97282. For subscription information call (800) 541-9498. ISBN: 1-57188-030-5 UPC: 0-66066-00221-1 Printed in Hong Kong

NORTH UMPQUA RIVER

(The Steamboat Area)

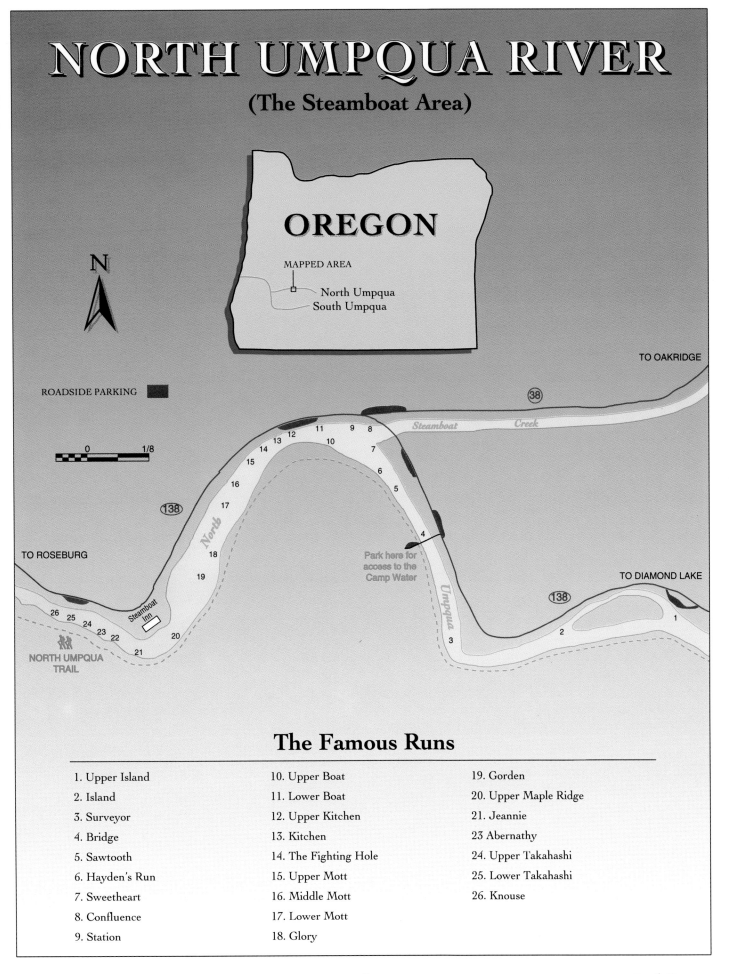

OREGON

MAPPED AREA

North Umpqua
South Umpqua

N

TO OAKRIDGE

ROADSIDE PARKING

(38)

Steamboat Creek

0   1/8

(138)

North

TO ROSEBURG

Park here for
access to the
Camp Water

TO DIAMOND LAKE

Umpqua

(138)

Steamboat Inn

NORTH UMPQUA TRAIL

The Famous Runs

1. Upper Island	10. Upper Boat	19. Gorden
2. Island	11. Lower Boat	20. Upper Maple Ridge
3. Surveyor	12. Upper Kitchen	21. Jeannie
4. Bridge	13. Kitchen	23 Abernathy
5. Sawtooth	14. The Fighting Hole	24. Upper Takahashi
6. Hayden's Run	15. Upper Mott	25. Lower Takahashi
7. Sweetheart	16. Middle Mott	26. Knouse
8. Confluence	17. Lower Mott	
9. Station	18. Glory	

NORTH UMPQUA

River Of Legend: The Storied North Umpqua

"No other river at the time so strongly defined steelhead fly fishing."
—Trey Combs, Steelhead Fly Fishing, *1992.*

"If we were to grab our rods and head for the pond, Frank would be out with his shotgun in no time," Joe quipped as we pulled into the driveway of Frank Moore's impressively picturesque log home nestled amongst the conifers high above the North Umpqua.

Indeed, a quiet little pond, its glassy surface only now sprinkled with increasingly fervent raindrops, spread through a little hollow across the narrow, gravel road from the Moore place. Frank's aquarium, this pond: He speaks of its hatches and its impressive trout as another man might speak of his intricate garden.

Not wanting a load of buckshot as my first introduction to Frank Moore, I decided it best that we simply knock on the front door. The cabin's solid door swung open while I wondered about the moose rack hanging above. Frank was precisely as I had expected: An older gentleman in years perhaps, but catlike in the ease of his movements. His intellect—his grasp of the issues surrounding his beloved North Umpqua—made itself felt almost at once.

For a brief moment, Frank Moore and Joe Howell shook hands and then embraced as if they hadn't seen each other in years, although weeks would have been more accurate. For that few seconds I saw a mutual respect, a deep friendship and admiration; I saw two men—two steelhead anglers—whose intertwined lives and long association had created a bond that transcended fishing, but a bond created by a magical river.

Inside the Moore's rustic cabin I found a history of the North Umpqua better than anything to be found on the written page: Joe Howell pointed out Zane Grey's wading boots, hanging from a peg on one wall. Romer Grey, Zane's son, gave the boots to Frank. Along the walls of the living room hung a multitude of photos of famous anglers past and present and massive bookshelves, filled to overflow, loomed above in the loft.

We sat for a few moments, sipping hot coffee while the raindrops beat against the living-room window. Frank's wife Jeanne arrived a few moments later, just back from a scouting trip in preparation for an upcoming wildflower show. I asked Jeanne about a few of the wildflowers I had stumbled upon during the last week's fishing, describing them rather badly but as best as I could remember. She patiently identified them for me despite my less-than-scientific descriptions.

A few days later I was visiting the Moore's once again. They possess a quality of attraction: You can't help but feel that your mere association with Frank and Jeanne will somehow broaden your horizons and widen your awareness. They are our link to the North Umpqua's days of glory, when the river had first gained world-wide attention and when the most incredible of steelhead ascended the most wild of streams.

Frank and Jeanne owned Steamboat Inn, beginning in 1957, when they bought the operation from Clarence Gordon. Nearly 30 years earlier, in 1929, Major Jordan Lawrence Mott set up a fishing camp on the river's south bank. The camp, comprised of

North Umpqua

Steamboat Inn, located on a bluff above the lower end of the famed "Camp Water," offers a long tradition of fine dining and well-appointed accommodations.

tent-cabins, stood on the rise overlooking the famous pools immediately below the confluence with Steamboat Creek. Sadly, Mott died in the spring of 1931 after only two summer seasons on the North Umpqua.

In those early days, visitors to the Mott Camp were ferried across the Boat Pool by Mott's guide and run-about, Zeke Allen. Even before Mott arrived, John Ewell had built several cabins on Canton Creek, which joins Steamboat Creek about a half mile from the latter stream's confluence with the North Umpqua. It was here that Clarence Gordon stayed on his initial visit to the North Umpqua in 1929.

In 1934, Gordon, with a forest service lease, started the camp that was soon to become the revered North Umpqua Lodge. Visitors arrived from all quarters, among them Ray Bergman, Claude Krieder and Clark C. Van Fleet, all of whom wrote of their experiences on this renowned river.

The famous author Zane Grey first visited the North Umpqua in 1932 and became enamored with the river's steelhead and wild settings. The Zane Grey stories have grown larger over the years, but one thing is certain: Grey brought an entourage with him in 1932, including a film-making crew headed by his eldest son Romer, his assistants and secretaries who assisted in Zane's writing and editing, several friends and relatives and a Japanese cook, George Takahashi, for whom Takahashi Riffle was named. In *Steelhead Fly Fishing*, which includes a wealth of historical information about those early days on the North Umpqua, Trey Combs relates the following: "Romer filmed comic relief, too. Little Takahashi would climb a tree and fly fish from a branch. As a technician, out of view of the camera, pulled violently on the line, Takahashi, a look of astonishment on his face, would come flying out of the tree and into the river. Presumably this was hysterical to everyone except the star."

Grey returned to the river each season until 1937, when he

apparently suffered a stroke one morning while sitting in the sun at his camp, which by then had been moved to Williams Creek in order to avoid the increasing crowds visiting Gordon's Lodge and fishing the Camp Water below Steamboat Creek. Grey died in southern California two years later.

By the late 1940s, Frank Moore, along with the well-known local guide Joe DeBernardi, were guiding Gordon's guests on the now-famous pools of the North Umpqua. But all was not well on this most-famous of steelhead streams, for in the early 1950s, the North Umpqua Highway was under construction, as was a hydro-electric project that would so adversely affect the fishing that Clarence Gordon was prompted to close his lodge in 1952. Gordon soon opened Steamboat Store on the river's north bank and later moved the operation to the present-day site of Steamboat Inn. The Moore's bought Steamboat Store in 1957.

During these same years—the late '40s and early '50s—concern was growing over the dwindling stocks of salmon and steelhead, urging the Roseburg Rod & Gun Club to push for a fly-fishing-only designation. In 1951, District game supervisor James Vaughn and Umpqua fish biologist William Pitney submitted to the game commission the regulation proposal to make the North Umpqua a fly-only river from Rock Creek to Soda Springs.

Initially, Frank Moore expressed concern over limiting access to this splendid river: He felt that a fly-only regulation would effectively prevent kids and elderly people from fishing the stream. At the urging of a few friends in the rod and gun club, Frank took his young son fly fishing on the North Umpqua's classic waters and at the age of five, little Frankie hooked his first steelhead. Frank was thus convinced. He would support the fly-only proposal, which was designed in essence and in fact to limit the effectiveness of sport fishing on the river and thus allow some measure of safe haven for salmon, steelhead and their smolts.

The Moore's built upon the tradition of Clarence Gordon's old North Umpqua Lodge. They built several cabins below the Inn and continued serving the Fisherman's Dinners each night at a half hour past sunset. Amongst their regular guests was one Ken Anderson, who devised the idea of forming a group of anglers who would guard the integrity of this renowned steelhead river. Stan Knouse came up with the name "Steamboaters." The Steamboaters today boast a membership of more than 300.

Trey Combs, in *Steelhead Fly Fishing*, says, "I believe that, were it not for the Steamboaters, the fly fishing-only section of river would have been lost long ago, logging would have destroyed the few fine spawning tributaries, and the native run of North Umpqua summer steelhead would be but a fine memory."

Many would agree with that statement. The Steamboaters

were (and are today) the most significant voice in the effort to protect and preserve the North Umpqua and its runs of anadromous fish. The organization long ago became an institution, an integral player in North Umpqua lore.

During the early 1980s another institution began, this one a fly shop located just below the deadline of the fly water and owned by Joe and Bonnie Howell. Joe grew up fishing the Umpqua and eventually moved from Roseburg to a beautiful, shaded property overlooking the river near the tiny town of Idleyld Park.

Joe Howell's Blue Heron Fly Shop occupies a converted wing of the house; a beautifully painted sign on the highway below guides you up the gravel driveway to the shop. Inside you find everything you could need during a visit to the North Umpqua, including fly bins full of Joe's favorite patterns.

Richard T. Grost

While his shop became an institution of sorts for North Umpqua anglers, Joe Howell's knowledge of the river has become widely appreciated. When he bought a new truck recently, I told him he would perhaps get a summer of fishing without worrying about those folks who habitually learn all Joe's favorite pools by driving around looking for Joe's vehicle parked along the highway.

"Maybe for a little while," he said, "but they will catch on fast."

Joe's fly tying skills are well known in the steelheading community and so too is his casting ability. Many anglers are said to be great casters, but to watch Joe Howell fish his river is a special treat: He can roll cast like a magician—a valuable skill on a river whose already-limited backcast room seems to shrink a little each season as the trees grow bigger. He mends line as accurately and precisely as anyone I have ever seen, swimming his fly expertly through the most narrow and most unreachable of places.

All of this he does while maintaining a cagey sense of humor: I was fast to a bruiser of a winter fish, which had run well down into the Boat Hole. When I finally figured the fish was beaten and was about to drag her into the frog-water, a softball-sized rock sailed over my head and splashed down like a brick. The steelhead screamed out into the pool again.

I turned around to catch Joe with a devilish grin on his face. "Thought you should get one more run out of her," he said.

Later that same day I was watching Joe guide his expertly placed roll casts through a narrow corridor of brush on an elegant little pool almost devoid of backcasting room. In an effort to create some semblance of a backcasting lane, someone had taken a saw to the large alders immediately behind Joe's casting station. Occasionally, during mid-stroke of a double roll cast, Joe's line would catch on a few overhanging alder branches.

After one of Joe's roll casts tore a few buds from an alder branch, I suggested that whoever did the cutting should have done a little better job of it. "You should ask Frank Moore about it," Joe suggested with a grin. "He's been known to create a casting lane or two over the years, though he probably wouldn't admit to it."

Frank has done more than just create a casting lane or two.

While talking with Frank and Jeanne one day, I was relating a story Walt Johnson told me about his first and only trip to the North Umpqua during the late '40s. At that time, a wood plank—a peer of sorts, extended out from the bank to the edge of what is called the Station or the Station Pool. Anglers could walk out to the end of the plank and fish the narrow, ledge-bound slot from a terribly advantageous position.

After I had related Walt Johnson's story of nearly stepping off the end of the plank and into the depths of the "Plank Pool" as it was often called then, Jeanne Moore gave me an ending for the tale, saying, "and we know someone who may have had something to do with removing that plank."

I was a little slow in grasping her meaning until I caught the little fox-like grin on Frank's face.

Only after I outright asked him what happened, did Frank relate the story of how late one evening he snuck down into the Plank Pool and removed the peer. "What did you do, just saw off the pilings?" I asked.

"No, I removed it by hand," Frank returned, "Had to wrestle around with that thing a bit, but I tore it out of there."

"Then they rebuilt it," offered Jeanne, "so Frank went down and tore it out of there a second time."

Frank recalled that "the plank was built a lot sturdier the second time, and it was about all I could do just to get it loosened up. I was down in the river pushing and pulling for all I was worth and the braces were creaking real loud until I finally got it free."

The plank builders must have realized that they'd been beaten, for the Plank Pool would never again bear the object of its name.

My first visit with the Moore's ended too soon on a rainy March afternoon. Frank escorted us out to my truck in the driveway, just across the road from the pond full of big trout.

"We had some really big ones," Frank said, "but someone poached them out of there."

By big, Frank meant rainbows in the eight-pound or better category.

Joe suggested that Frank might be well-served to find someone to guard the pond on those frequent occasions when the Moore's were away. Perhaps Frank could prevent further depredations that way.

"Well," Frank said, "I think I know who did it."

That same fox-like grin crept across Frank's face and his eyes twinkled ever so slightly. I wouldn't want to be the party responsible for raiding Frank Moore's fish pond.

***

Joe Howell and his Blue Heron Fly Shop have become institutions on the North Umpqua River.
The shop is located just upstream from the town of Idleyld Park.

River Of Character:
Learning The North Umpqua

"Next morning I found the Umpqua to be a totally different stream. . .and more difficult to figure out. There are stretches of foaming white-water riffles, narrow glassy chutes and glides separated by great boulders and ledges, and between at wide intervals are great, deep, bubble-shot pools. It is a wild and mysterious and appealing stream, shouting and murmuring by turn down the deep verdant canyon. And I wondered just where to try my fly."

—Claude M. Kreider, Steelhead, 1948.

Completely deserted on this late September Wednesday, Bogus Creek Campground offered shade and a place to snooze for the hot part of the day.

I had just drifted off toward that dream state where every cast tempts a steelhead from the Umpqua's emerald waters when the shrill cry of a Stellar's Jay jolted me back to the real world. I'm not sure who was more startled—me or the jay that had landed on my left foot as I lounged on my army cot. This jay had seen a few generous humans before, judging by the fact that he jumped only as far as the nearest fir branch. I reached for a half-full box of cheese nips and tossed a few of the bright orange crackers toward the base of the tree. The bird pounced on them instantly, as if cheese nips were a favorite. Two more of the stately blue jays assaulted my offerings.

Before I could again doze in the afternoon heat, the resonant cry of a woodpecker echoed through the tall evergreens. After a while, a blur of black and white sailed through the dense understory of maple and perched upside down on a sweeping branch. This elegant pileated woodpecker deserved a closer look, so I dug out the binoculars. On cue, the crow-sized woodpecker glided to the fir tree whose shade I was now enjoying. Clinging to the trunk just 20 feet away from me, the male pileated assured me of a good look.

My camera, of course, was buried in fishing gear in the truck. Another pileated woodpecker made its entrance, this one a female. Together they darted back to the oak tree. Soon they were joined by two sapsuckers—the brilliant red ones common to the west slope of the Cascades.

Every time I drifted off to sleep, some new forest denizen would announce its arrival. A flock of chickadees, varied thrushes, several pine squirrels and a blacktail doe that crossed the highway and ambled through camp as if she owned the joint. Perhaps she did at that.

Consequently I gave up on the sleep idea and set about tying a few flies. My fly boxes always end up empty one way or another. Sometimes I retire the successful flies, occasionally I'll lose one to a fish or to a tree; most of the time I just give too many away to fellow anglers and leave myself with scant selections. I tied three Spawning Purple's that afternoon and just like that the time had arrived to don the waders again.

For a day and a half now the steelhead had managed to befuddle me, but this evening would change that I surmised. Confidence plays a vital role in steelhead fly fishing and the longer I go without hooking a fish, the more strongly I believe I am destined to do so on forthcoming casts.

I choose a favorite pool upstream from Wright Creek. I fished through from top to bottom without touching a fish. As always though, I lost myself in the sheer magnificence of this splendid river: towering douglas firs leaning out over the water like sentinels on duty and curious water ouzels diving under water and then flittering to the nearest rock before announcing their appar-

The author whips up a Spawning Purple for the afternoon fishing on the upper river.

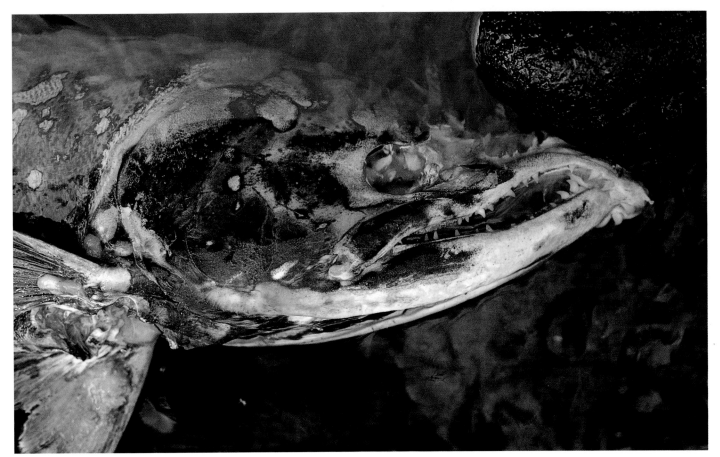

Dead Chinook salmon below Marster's Bridge.

ent joy with the most melodious of songs; The moss-cloaked river boulders and the orange-tinged maples reflected in the Umpqua's glorious waters.

In many ways, the North Umpqua is all steelhead rivers: As it gouges a path through steep canyon walls, the North Umpqua creates every imaginable kind of steelhead water and all of it in abundance. From glass-smooth tailouts and choppy runs, to gliding bedrock-rimmed chutes and deep pocket water, the North Umpqua offers something for everyone and in doing so becomes unique unto itself.

The magnitude of the river is impressive, not so much for the 33 miles set aside for fly fishing, but for the countless steelhead lies found through this section and for the diversity of their natures. In one place you scramble down the steepest of inclines, picking your way through riprap and blackberries, always just one wrong step away from getting to the bottom much more quickly than antici-pated. When you  finally emerge at river's edge, you find all your efforts will yield but a single cast-ing station—a single rock scarred with cleat marks from sea-sons past.

A handful of casts might cover this pool and then you are left with the prospect of renegotiating the highway embankment. The next pool offers stark contrast: You park alongside the highway on a gravel pullout and follow a well-worn path through a canopy of maples and douglas firs to reach a sprawling pool whose cob-blestone bottom is entirely wadeable from top to tailout. An hour and dozens of casts pass before you have entirely covered this ele-gant pool.

The North Umpqua is renowned for its treacherous wading, but an angler could spend an entire season fishing just those pools where sure footing is abundant; conversely, one could spend that same season negotiating pools where a thorough dunking is near-ly as sure as the morning sun. In fact, I often think one ought to just sit down in the river first thing in the morning just to get it over with.

The fly water begins at the angling deadline about a half mile downstream from Soda Springs Dam. Here the river is character-ized by a steep gradient and tumbling pocket water. Lightly fished, this upper end of the fly water is accessed by either Boulder Creek Trail or by a forest service spur that crosses the river just below the dam on a precarious little bridge. A number of steelhead negotiate this upper section of the fly water and some are taken each season; most of the fish—summer steelhead and especially winter steelhead—end their upriver journey's short of Soda Springs Dam.

A couple miles below the dam, Boulder Flat Campground and Eagle Rock Campground offer access to a handful of steelhead pools and runs. Following Hwy. 138 downstream from Eagle Rock Campground, you cross the river at Marster's Bridge. During the fall, Chinook salmon can be observed on their spawn-ing beds along the edges of the wide gravel flat around the corner from the bridge.

Forest Service Road No. 4770 heads off to the south just above Marster's Bridge and a short distance up this gravel road lies the uppermost trailhead for the trail system (Mott Trail) that follows the river's south bank. Anglers willing to hike this trail can fish pools not accessible from the highway side of the river.

From Marster's Bridge to Dry Creek, anglers can access the river from either the trail on the south bank or from the highway, now on the north bank. Below, Dry Creek some of the more productive pools require a laborious (and at times treacherous) plunge over a long, steep grade off the highway embankment. Just over a mile below Dry Creek, the river sweeps through a long bend, hence the name of Horseshoe Bend Campground.

Between Horseshoe Bend and Apple Creek campgrounds, some three miles of river are characterized by a steep climb down to water's edge and widely varied steelhead runs. Above Horseshoe Bend, the North Umpqua's gradient lessons some, and long, wadeable pools become more prevalent. Mott Trail follows the south bank through most of the fly water and, in a few instances, can provide access to pools and runs that are difficult if not impossible to fish from the highway side. Some sections of this trail hang precipitously from the canyon wall and leave little if any access to the river below. This is especially true downstream from the Camp Water. Nonetheless, the Mott Trail allows more adventurous anglers to escape the crowds that often accumulate along the highway.

About four miles below Apple Creek, just around the corner from Island Campground, Mott Bridge crosses high over the river a short distance upstream from Steamboat Creek. Anglers can park just across the bridge and follow a short section of the Mott Trail that leads to the famed Camp Water.

So named because of its proximity to Mott's Camp (later Clarence Gordon's North Umpqua Lodge) that once stood on the south bank, the Camp Water is comprised of a number of revered, well-known steelhead pools. At the top, just below Mott Bridge is the Bridge Hole. From atop the bridge, one can often spot steelhead holding in the channel between reefs of ledgerock. Below the Bridge Hole, the main current flows through a chute bordered on both sides by sheer ledges. This long, narrow glide is called Sawtooth, its name deriving from a section of sharp-edged, jagged reef that is famed for its ability to separate a steelhead from the angler on the other end.

Just below Sawtooth is Hayden's Run. Toward the highway side and just above the confluence of Steamboat Creek is Sweetheart, followed by the Confluence Hole and then the Station Hole. The latter, named for the forest service station that once stood atop the bank, was also called the "Plank Pool" because of a wooden platform that was built out over the water enabling anglers to position themselves for an easy time of it fishing this gliding reef-bound run.

Below Station, the river surges through a short rapids before fanning out into the most magnificent of steelhead pools, this one known as the Boat Hole. Upper Boat (or "Top of The Boat") is a narrow chute above the main pool; Middle Boat and Lower Boat sprawl out over a tremendous cobblestone bar,

Mott Bridge, a historic landmark that was completed in 1936, spans the river above the Camp Water. Across the bridge lies the parking lot and trailhead that leads anglers to the famed pools of the North Umpqua, including Station, Boat, Kitchen, Mott, Glory, and Gordon.

14

Looking down through the lower extent of the Camp Water, which Trey Combs called "the most celebrated waters in all of steelhead fly fishing."

studded here and there with bedrock reefs.

Major Jordon Lawrence Mott, who set up the first camp on the river's south bank in 1929, hired Zeke Allen, a local guide, as his cook and assistant at the fly fishing camp that first year. Visitors would signal the camp via a bell on the north bank and Allen would then ferry them across on a rowboat, hence the pool's name.

At its lower reaches, the Boat Hole tails into a narrowing chute of bedrock reefs, forming the Kitchen Pool, so named because it was overlooked by Mott's kitchen tent. Later, a trail led from Clarence Gordon's dining hall down the bank to the Kitchen Pool.

Below Kitchen, the flow glides through a series of ledgerock pools: The Fighting Hole, Upper, Middle and Lower Mott, Glory Hole and Gordon.

From the Bridge Hole to Gordon and beyond, the flow glides over and through ledgerock reefs and channels, forming what Trey Combs called "the most celebrated waters in all of steelhead fly fishing." (Combs, *Steelhead Fly Fishing*, 1991).

These storied pools continue around the next bend, below Steamboat Inn: Maple Ridge, Jeannie, Abernathy, Takahashi (named for Zane Grey's Japanese cook, George Takahashi), Knouse. Further downstream one finds The Ledges, Tree Pool, Divide Pool, Williams Creek Riffle, The Log Pool and Discovery Pool. The popular Archie, a deep reef-bound tailout, lies some half a mile downstream from The Discovery Pool, with ample fishable water in between. Another mile or so downriver is Bogus Creek Campground and from there to the lower boundary of the fly water (about 12 miles), the Umpqua offers countless pools and runs where steelhead lie during both the summer and winter seasons.

The popular pools are easy to find: Look for pullouts along the highway. These same pools generally feature the same worn path of rocks scarred from wading cleats. Hence if you find yourself wondering which rock is *the* casting station, just look for the one decorated with cleat scars.

Throughout the North Umpqua (and especially from Apple Creek to the lower end of the fly water) dry fly anglers will find a number of perfectly smooth tailouts where a skating fly might bring an explosive boil first thing in the morning or at last light—maybe any time of day when the river is uncrowded.

Fishing The North Umpqua

"The roar of its mighty voice fills the canyon of its passage from source to junction as it tumbles down the rough, boulder-strewn cleft carved by its journey. A mile of fishing along its banks is a very real test of endurance as you snake your way over the folds in the bedrock, scramble onto jagged reefs and cross huge piles of rubble."
—*Clark C. Van Fleet,* Steelhead to a Fly, *1951*

The outer end of a fly line appeared behind a screen of alders on a small island downstream. I watched the line unfurl and watched the fly disappear instantly into the glassy waters of one of the Umpqua's many classic runs. Forrest had found a crossing to the mid-river island.

I fished my way through the tailout that had begged my attention: The river folded gracefully around a small horseshoe bend and then cut through a channel whose near edge formed from a sheer face of ledgerock and whose far bank offered a steep cobblestone bank. Dead in the middle stood a lone truck-sized boulder, below which a narrow tailout smoothed the riffled waters before they plunged over a gentle waterfall into the pool below.

No fish humored me from this lovely and varied pool so I went in search of Forrest's path across the river to the island. The river opposite the island lay completely out of view, but judging from the emphatic manner in which Forrest's line was jumping out over the first pool, I guessed what lay beyond must indeed be exceptional water.

A big log jam offered a chance, albeit an iffy one. I tested a huge old deadfall with one foot, then jumped on and tightroped my way over the kind of white water one wouldn't want to experience up close.

The other side of the island offered three prime runs—Forrest was busy with the uppermost pool—a classic head-throat-tailout job whose boulder-clad banks melded into the shadows cast by tremendous old Douglas firs that leaned out over the river.

Forrest Maxwell fishes through one of the North Umpqua's exquisite steelhead runs, this one toward the lower end of the fly water. It is pools like this one that seem to suggest that this magnificent river was designed with the fly angler in mind.

Parts of the Camp Water remain fishable even at high water. Here Joe Howell fishes Upper Boat.

Immediately below the tailout, the main current gathered momentum and glanced off a rock face on the far side of the channel. From here the currents rebounded back to the middle of the river and fanned out over a narrow cobblestone bar. I leave this run for Forrest and choose the next good water below. Here a large boulder divided the current, with the outer channel forming a narrow, smooth seam that looked as fishy as anything I had fished all evening.

Utterly dumbfounded that neither of us took a fish from these elegant steelhead pools, Forrest led the way back across the island. Prompted along by an angry swarm of yellow jackets, two of whom notched their guns at my expense, we took the first reasonable path back to the highway side of the river. We scrambled up a steep, timbered embankment to the highway (Umpqua anglers spend lots of time scrambling up and down steep embankments).

On the way back to our lonesome encampment at Eagle Rock Campground, we pulled into a narrow turnout above Marster's Bridge and plunged over the side to fish a one-cast hole that looked too good to pass by. Forrest suggested I go ahead and fish the tiny slot; I suggested he go ahead; He insisted I fish it; I insisted he fish it; Rapidly approaching darkness insisted we both end the debate over who would get the shot, so I eased into chest-deep water, made a 12-foot cast to a bathtub-sized slot bordered by a ridge of bedrock that concealed my approach. Then I watched as a silvery shadow glided effortlessly toward the surface and inhaled my Spawning Purple.

That evening was classic North Umpqua: We cast over every conceivable water type in half a day's fishing, from classic pools to ledgerock runs to glassy smooth tailouts. When we finally found a biter, she was a visual one—a fish whose deliberate take was starkly and stunningly visible.

The previous evening we had taken three fish; this day we hooked two. Tomorrow might prove fishless or might be a steelheading day of a lifetime. No matter how many fish, if any, come to the fly, however, every day spent casting over the North Umpqua's resplendent steelhead pools is a day not easily forgotten.

A Steelheader's Graduate School

The North Umpqua's magnificent beauty, coupled with its complete array of water types, makes this river an experience unto itself. One run is lined with massive shelves of slab bedrock, yet around the next bend lies a classic cobblestone pool. Below this a gliding run slices through sheer stone ridges and then the river fans out into a pool combining all these elements.

Indeed, anglers can choose whatever kind of water pleases them. Those who seek the classic pools will find plenty of water to keep them busy. Anglers who like the small, out-of-the-way runs and slots can fish such places all day long. Some North Umpqua regulars fish only the Camp Water; others ignore this section entirely until late in the season when the crowds depart. Still others stick to the confines of the upper river while a few loners seek only the glassy tailouts where lurking steelhead might chase skating flies

Your first trip to the North Umpqua might leave you wondering just where to begin: After all, as you drive upstream from the tiny village of Idleyld, you are treated to teasing glimpses of different sections of the river. You know a thing or two about reading steelhead water so early on you begin to realize the magnitude of this river: Every time you round a bend and view a new section of river you are greeted by fishy-looking runs, pools and tailouts. Perhaps you begin to wonder just which of these places holds fish.

At precisely the moment such thoughts cross your mind—at that moment when you begin to wonder whether you should keep driving, go back to that last stretch or stop right here and fish—you had better do the latter. Just stop at the next fishy-looking section of river, string a rod and get personal with the North Umpqua. Only then will you begin to appreciate this gracefully wild river and the opportunity it offers.

Certainly I could describe to you many of my favorite pools and runs, but to do so would be to rob you of one of the most treasured and intriguing experiences offered by the North Umpqua: the opportunity to discover for yourself the mysteries of one of our most cherished steelhead waters. For ten years I made only the occasional trip to the North Umpqua, until two years ago when happenstance placed me within a two-and-a-half hour drive of the river. I quickly became enamored with the North Umpqua, driving that two and half hours virtually every week for three months during the summer and three months during the winter.

Sometimes I stay for a week; other times just for the day. At all times the drive is worthwhile and so intriguing and intoxicating is this river that in the course of a single autumn I spent more days fishing the North Umpqua than I had spent on the deschutes in three seasons.

An angler tight to a chrome summer steelhead. Richard T. Grost photo

The author with a North Umpqua hatchery steelhead taken on the upper river. The presence of hatchery steelhead in the river is a topic of some debate for all but the Oregon Department of Fish and Wildlife, which doesn't seem willing to question its own policy regarding the management of wild fish and introduced hatchery stock.

Still I have much to learn and much to discover about this stream: I'm lousy with names of places—I tend to forget the labels placed on runs and pools and instead remember the curl of the water around my waders, the contour of the bottom, the vibrant surroundings and the occasional grab of a steelhead. On more than one occasion I've dropped in on Joe Howell and described the water I'd been fishing that day to which he always responds first by telling me what the pool is called and then by recollecting a story of his own from that very place—the memories of past deeds and adventures always fresh on his mind.

I've dropped in on Joe during the worst of water conditions, when the winter flows run so high that virtually nothing is even remotely fishable. And still the drive is worthwhile and Joe never seems surprised that I knock on his door on those days when no sane being would don waders and string a rod. From his many seasons on the North Umpqua, Joe Howell understands the way this river can overwhelm one's soul and intoxicate one's mind.

Indeed it is the process of discovery that I and many others find so intriguing about fly fishing in general and about the North Umpqua in particular. This river leaves much to discovery and indeed those who insist on maps and charts and descriptions and guides necessarily divest themselves of the North Umpqua's most abundant quality, the element of pleasant surprise and endless fascination.

The North Umpqua will mesmerize you: As you cast your way through a pool, you begin to lose all sense of time; all sense of urgency. This pool looks too good not to produce a fish and you soon begin to appreciate an important fact about the North Umpqua: During the peak of the summer run, virtually every good piece of holding water will contain at least one steelhead and many will harbor substantial numbers of fish.

Perhaps the storied Camp Water at Steamboat is your ultimate goal, but as you drive upriver from the west or downstream from the east, you will no doubt begin to appreciate the extent and diversity of the North Umpqua. With so much beautiful steelhead water available, one can very easily fish away an entire day or an entire week or an entire season without ever setting foot on the well-worn course through the pools at the Camp Water.

When you do visit the Camp Water—which every fly angler should do at least once—you can negotiate your way through the pools simply by following the cleat marks on the rocks. Left by generations of anglers, the scarred path through these most prestigious of steelhead pools will lead you on a magical journey that begs reflection on steelheader's past and the fish they hooked in these fabled waters.

Perhaps you will begin at the Confluence Hole where Steamboat Creek joins the North Umpqua and then fish through Station Hole before entering the sprawling pool below. This is the Boat Hole (or Upper Boat and Lower Boat). Lower Boat becomes Upper Kitchen and then you reach the Kitchen Hole itself, a gliding, ledgerock-bound run and tailout whose classic proportions and elegant beauty defy accurate description.

In 1951, Clark C. Van Fleet wrote a little-known but exquisite book titled *Steelhead to a Fly*. Of the Kitchen (so named because it was visible from the dining hall at the old lodge owned by Clarence Gordon), he wrote:

> The trail from the dining room [of Clarence Gordon's lodge on the south bank] leads down the sharp bank to the Kitchen Pool, where the quiet water mirrors swift reflections of the shining heights as you step out on the shingle. Approach the head of the reef through the deepening water where the trough of the channel shows deep before you. The grip of the current will be surprisingly strong for such apparent placidity.

Your fly drops lightly at the edge of the farther reefhead and makes a slight riffle crossing the slick, barely submerged. A thorough search of the now widening trough brings no response . . . The slab under you shoals until a more abrupt rise gives you dry footing. The far stone ridge breaks into two parts with a deep pocket between the sunken portion and the exposed hump beyond. This is the first hot spot, so you cover the water well from the reef to the shallow ledges on your own side; gradually you extend your line until you are flicking the dry projection on the far side. Still no response . . . a few steps and you repeat the exhaustive search.

The channel widens to a bay as the opposing shoal breaks off abruptly and the flow speeds up for the long chute to the lower riffle. At the very tail, the noses of three bedrock reefs somewhat divide the flow. In front of these is the final sure lie in the Kitchen.

As your fly crosses the bulge of the first reef, there is a deep swirl, a shock on your line, a whirr of your reel to announce the first steelhead. The thrill warms you like wine, the tingle of delight vibrates your rod as the rush ends in a powerful leap that sends a circling wave across the pool.

Van Fleet's description of the Kitchen Pool is as accurate today as it was more than four decades ago when Clarence Gordon operated his lodge on the south bank of the river. Indeed, all of the pools collectively called the Camp Water remain little changed from season to season and decade to decade. The fish occupy the same lies as they have for years and one cannot help but reflect on the Clarence Gordon's, Major Mott's, Clark Van Fleet's, Zane Grey's and other notables whose cleated impressions mingle with those of thousands of other anglers upon the bedrock reefs of the Camp Water

Below the Kitchen Hole, the river glides through a quickening channel and fans into Upper Mott, Middle Mott and Lower Mott Pools. By now morning has melded into noon-time and the remainder of the day is easily spent fishing these graceful pools. Some distance below Lower Mott, you fish through the Glory Hole and Gordon. If time and desire permit you might then follow the path downriver to the pools overlooked by Steamboat Inn: Upper Maple Ridge, Maple Ridge, Jeannie, Abernathy, Takahashi and Knouse.

Having fished through this most cherished of steelhead water, you might then return to Mott Bridge and gaze down into the Bridge Hole, a glassy run whose sides are guarded by ledges of bedrock. In quick succession below the Bridge Hole is the lengthy Sawtooth, Hayden's Run and Sweetheart, all just upstream from the confluence with Steamboat Creek. Climbing over the rail, you saunter across the bridge: Upstream lies the Surveyor Hole.

Summer or winter, steelhead return to these pools each season. And each of these revered pools offers something new and different, from the narrow curling chute at the Confluence Hole to the sprawling breadth of the Boat Hole to the deep green channels of the Mott Pool.

Yet even in all their classic resplendence, these pools called the Camp Water only hint at the full magnitude of the North Umpqua's 33-mile-long fly-only section. For miles below and miles above the Steamboat area, the North Umpqua gouges a course through solid bedrock, cascading through a deep canyon and offering fly anglers the opportunity to cast elegant steelhead flies over the most diverse of watery terrain: In one pool you are confined to a single large rock, from which you will lengthen your line some four or five feet on each successive cast until your fly has covered the sweet part of the pool; immediately below you find a classic, wadeable pool where each cast steers a course through new waters, where a steelhead might be forthcoming on the first short cast at the pool's head or the last offering deep into the tailout.

In many places, your backcast must dart expertly through the understory of maple and alders; in other pools you must elevate the backstroke to clear the highway embankment immediately behind. Round the next bend, however, and you find a run where the cast can blossom to its full grace and elegance with no obstacles to steer its course. Here you stand high above the water and cast a hundred feet; there you wade in behind a boulder and dabble a ten-foot cast. In many ways, the North Umpqua is all steelhead rivers wrapped into one and in that sense, this graceful and challenging river cannot help but prepare you for other streams in other places.

Looking upstream from atop Mott Bridge.

North Umpqua

Fishing The Summer Run

By June, summer steelhead begin to accumulate in the fly-water section of the North Umpqua and by mid July, they are present in numbers that attract attention from anglers. The peak of the run occurs during August and fishing remains productive through September and October.

During this time frame, however, the weather pattern changes from the unpredictable nature of early summer to the hot days of July and August to the increasing clouds and autumn cooling of October. The high water might roar through the river's canyon through June only to dwindle to a comparative trickle by August. During late summer, in fact, the North Umpqua sometimes runs low enough that the water warms to the point where steelhead and steelhead anglers alike will find things rather unpleasant.

During these periods of low, warm water, steelhead often act sulky and seem uninclined to move for the fly. At the same time, anglers discard the waders in exchange for shorts, heavy socks and the usual cleated boots. The fish can still be had, however, by those who fish the early morning and late evening hours and who spend the mid-afternoon casting over the river's many shaded pools and runs.

Indeed, despite the occasional bouts with low, warm water, August remains the most popular month on the North Umpqua. Vacationers from afar can set up camp at any of numerous campgrounds; locals try to hide from them, fishing out-of-the-way places and fishing popular pools early, late and mid-week.

By late August, the North Umpqua can at times be a busy river, especially for those who stick to the Camp Water in the vicinity of Steamboat. Arrive a month previous, however, and one might cast over empty pools and untouched tailouts during the pleasant mornings and quiet evenings of mid-week July days.

The fishing holds up through the early and mid-fall, with September and early October being decidedly pleasant and colorful times on the river. The maples adorn themselves in their full autumn regalia of yellows, golds, oranges and reds, offering poetic contrast to the steep canyon walls cloaked in the dark green of firs, cedars, pines and hemlock.

The North Umpqua's summer steelhead are a remarkable strain of fish. They habitually use the river's bedrock reefs to separate themselves from attached fly anglers. Fish of seven and eight pounds are common; 10- to 15-pound steelhead are present in reasonable numbers and a handful of 20-pound bruisers cross the ladders at Winchester Dam each summer.

Typically, some 50 to 75 percent of these fish are of hatchery origin and can be identified as such by their fin clips. These hatchery fish come entirely from North Umpqua brood stock: The Oregon Department of Fish and Wildlife traps steelhead at Rock Creek and milks these fish to raise the smolts that will be returned to the river at about eight inches in length. Brood-stock steelhead are selected more-or-less at random to assure genetic diversity and they are accumulated throughout the summer run in an effort to assure diversity in the timing of future returns.

Currently, 165,000 of these hatchery-reared smolt are allocated for release into the North Umpqua (see table on facing page). Naturally, mortality is high. According to ODFW biologist Dave Loomis, about a third of the smolts are released at Baker Park. This group is selected from the largest of the hatchery smolts available that year. The remaining smolt are released at Rock Creek and below the town of Glide at Whistler's Bend.

Upon their return from the Pacific these hatchery fish will hold for a time at their release sites. However, there appears to be no link between the release site of a steelhead smolt and the place where that fish will eventually end up in the river system.

Steamboat Creek summer steelhead. Richard T. Grost photo

North Umpqua River
Hatchery Steelhead Smolt Releases

Brood Year	Year Released	Number Released	Release Sites
1994	1995	164,500	Baker Park, Rock Cr., Whistler Bend
1993	1994	75,134	(major losses due to disease)
1992	1993	127,531	Baker Park, Rock Cr., Whistler Bend
1991	1992	176,730	Steamboat Flats, Rock Cr., Whistler Bend
1990	1991	171,827	"
1989	1990	152,242	"
1988	1989	91,862	"
1987	1988	178,260	"
1986	1987	178,204	"
1985	1986	172,241	"

In 1994, 4,710 summer steelhead crossed Winchester Dam, 2,599 of them wild fish. A majority of the North Umpqua's wild summer steelhead will spawn in the Steamboat and Canton Creek drainages (along the lines of 70 percent), with smaller contingents reproducing in several other tributaries. In fact, according to Dave Loomis, the majority of the remaining 25 or 30 percent of wild fish that don't ascend Steamboat Creek will spawn in the tributaries upriver. Amongst summer-run fish, little if any spawning occurs in the river proper (except in the closed area just below Soda Springs Dam). Loomis also notes that there exists strong evidence of some successful spawning of hatchery summer steelhead.

The final counts for summer steelhead passage over Winchester Dam between 1970 and 1994 are given in the table at the right. According to punchcard data, anglers on the upper North Umpqua caught an average of 4,167 summer steelhead each season between 1984-85 and 1993.

A pair of steelhead look for spawning gravel above one of the log sills installed below Soda Springs Dam.

Summer Steelhead Counts at Winchester Dam, North Umpqua River, 1970-94

Year	Wild	Hatchery	Total
1970	2,727	12,853	15,580
1971	2,509	13,676	16,185
1972	3,159	10,573	13,732
1973	2,932	6,172	9,104
1974	3,875	4,547	8,422
1975	4,189	4,957	9,146
1976	2,736	3,969	6,705
1977	5,153	4,588	9,741
1978	3,766	5,625	9,391
1979	5,689	5,251	10,940
1980	5,262	5,032	10,294
1981	4,267	2,053	6,320
1982	3,397	2,213	5,610
1983	3,301	905	4,206
1984	8,333	5,817	14,150
1985	7,499	7,658	15,157
1986	7,743	11,999	19,742
1987	5,388	15,337	20,725
1988	3,800	11,524	15,324
1989	3,602	8,906	12,508
1990	2,986	7,590	10,576
1991	2,534	2,339	4,873
1992	1,650	2,126	3,776
1993	2,931	2,483	5,414
1994	2,599	2,111	4,710

As with any steelhead river where counts taken at a fish ladder are available, angling pressure will be heaviest during years with strong runs and proportionately less heavy during lean seasons. Joe Howell relates that during the heavy runs of the mid-80s the running joke was that you had better pack along a boulder in your truck so you would have something to stand on—the river was that crowded. The more sparse runs of recent years have attracted fewer people. Indeed, for many North Umpqua regulars, a sparse summer run means a lot less people with whom to compete and is thus not so terrible.

Even during such lean runs, steelhead will occupy all the same pools and by late summer each good piece of holding water is likely to rest at least one fish. In many of the North Umpqua's pools, mid-day allows you ample opportunity to spot fish in the clear water. Sometimes, in fact, you can watch how a steelhead reacts (or fails to react) to your fly. Unfortunately, these visible fish attract the wrong kind of attention at times from anglers who believe that any fish they can spot is one they can catch—no matter what method must ultimately be employed.

Certainly many visible fish will prove receptive to the fly. Those that don't, however, are all too often subjected to increasingly desperate measures: First an angler tries the classic approach with either a skated dry fly or a swinging wet fly. Most anglers will switch flies a few times in an effort to determine if the fish has a preference; then they might try a sink-tip line. Perhaps this fish will "wake up" later; perhaps not. But the steelhead's refusal to move for successive attempts with different flies hardly justifies additional attempts in the form of cast-after-cast-after-cast with nymph and indicator or bombarding the pool with rocks in an effort to antagonize and enliven a fish deserving of whatever rest it can get.

More importantly, these sighted fish on the North Umpqua offer an opportunity quite rare in steelhead fly fishing: An angler—or a companion watching from the highway embankment above—can sometimes watch the fish take the fly. These are rare and precious moments, when a silvery ghost ascends from the depths and in a seemingly unhurried moment inhales the swinging fly for an angler whose hands are suddenly trembling with anticipation.

One of the author's favorite summer-run pools below the Camp Water. This small run typifies classic steelhead water amidst some of the most elegant scenery to be found on any steelhead river—the North Umpqua boasts many such pools.

This bright late fall summer run took the author's Spawning Purple pattern. Ken Hanley photo

Tackle And Flies For The Summer Run

Rods of ten feet or so will help elevate your backcast in those many places on the North Umpqua where the line must clear the highway embankment or shoreline trees and shrubs. Eight and nine-weight rods are most popular and for good reason: The typical North Umpqua steelhead is a tenacious beast when stuck in the jaw with an angler's hook.

Many pools are fit for Spey rods, but use discretion. Some of those same pools where backcasting room is at a premium also lack any suitable shoreline where the long rod might beach a fish.

A floating line will serve most of your needs during the North Umpqua's summer run season, although a sink-tip comes in handy in some of the deeper pools and during occasional periods of higher water. Don't be bashful about spooling on the backing as you may well need all of it with a particularly hot North Umpqua fish.

Traditional steelhead wet flies will serve you well on the North Umpqua. Amongst the more popular patterns are the following: Skunks, Green-Butt Skunks, Black Gordon, Purple Peril, Umpqua Special, Cumming's Special, Brad's Brat, Steelhead Muddler (wet) and others. For what it's worth, my personal favorites are the Spawning Purple, Maxwell's Purple Matuka, skunk and Brad's Brat. The first two of these flies account for the majority of steelhead I take on each of the streams I fish and have proven as effective on the North Umpqua as anywhere else.

Skating flies are popular on the river's smooth glides and tailouts. Some favorites include Bombers, Dry Muddlers, October Caddis and Stonefly patterns, as well as several local favorites developed by Joe Howell. Every once in a while, a steelhead is taken on a dead-drift dry fly, especially late in the season when the big orange *Dicosmoecus* caddis (October Caddis) are in abundance.

Lastly, North Umpqua anglers should choose their wading gear with foresight: Cleated boots or sandals are a must. During the hottest part of summer, one might opt for shorts or long pants instead of waders; during the fall, neoprenes will fight the chill of early morning and evening. Either way—and it bears repeating—cleated soles are mandatory.

Fishing The Winter Run

Only shin-deep, the torrent of water adjacent to the top of the Boat Hole was nearly unwadeable in the high water of an April afternoon. Carefully I picked my way across the gravel to a position from which I could get a good downstream angle for the swinging fly.

A sinking shooting head carried my Orange Heron fly into the edge of the white water at the run's far side. A cross-stream cast allowed time for the fly to sink before coming under tension and from there the swing was slow and deep. The third such cast met with a violent surge and I was fast to a steelhead that I was sure would go 15 pounds.

In an instant the fish "went over" and headed for places down-river. Clumsily I splashed ashore to seek a better vantage from which to battle this beast whose initial run had cleaned me of 35 feet of fly line, 100 feet of running line and a fair shake of backing—and whom showed no sign of capitulating.

I reached Lower Boat about the same time the steelhead was seeking Upper Kitchen and I figured I'd better stand my ground here or watch one of those fiendish reefs of bedrock divest me of this monster. An unexpected rushing leap sounded like a bowling ball being tossed in the water and this just as I had recovered a few feet of backing. Off the fish went again; again I held my ground. My shooting head seemed unreasonably far away when the fish finally decided to calm down some.

Then it was a simple matter of bringing her in—taking up line when she rested and giving in to her increasingly short bursts. I

finally worked her into shallow water, at which point Joe Howell tossed a big rock in her direction just to get things stirred up again. "I do that to everybody," he said with that sly grin of his.

Again I dragged her shoreward. Not so big as I had thought, but still a nine or ten pound North Umpqua winter fish, as perfectly proportioned as any steelhead one could dream up. The barbless 3/0 popped free as I steered the fish into the frogwater and she glided back into the glacial-green depths: A steelhead to be cherished always, for despite the high flows, she came to an elegant fly on this most elegant of rivers.

A week later I was fishing through the Camp Water with Forrest Maxwell, with whom I share many days afield each year. As luck would have it, my efforts were again rewarded, but this time by the biggest steelhead I had ever hooked. The fish made three rather slow, but unbelievably heavy runs and then decided to swim upstream and take up refuge on the bottom. From that point I might as well have been doing battle with a giant Chinook salmon in tide-water because that is exactly what this ordeal felt like.

Initially, Forrest had been standing by, pointing out places where I might beach the fish, but when he saw the bend in my nine-weight rod and saw how the tip bounced every time the fish flared it gills, his demeanor changed a little. The realization that had come over me already was just now dawning on him: This was no small fish and if I was to have any chance of landing him I'd better be prepared for an hour-long affair.

No amount of pressure would budge the fish, which was con-tently holding fast in about four feet of water. I tried walking upstream and down and changing the angles this way succeeded

Despite recent trends in steelhead fly fishing, winter fish respond well to the classic wet-fly swing, especially when the fly is presented on a sink-tip line.

On the highway shoulder downstream from Steamboat Creek, this sign explains the name Steamboat.

only in nudging the fish to swim, ever so deliberately, a few yards upstream, where he again held fast.

I began to worry that the fish had entered one of the many crevices in the reefs of solid bedrock, a position from which he could do all sorts of damage without much effort. Hence I had just decided that my best course of action was to wade right out there and try to scare the fish into a long run, which I hoped would be the beginning of his undoing. At precisely that moment the fly pulled free and somewhere in the Umpqua's green-tinged winter flows that leviathan went about his upriver odyssey.

Forrest was quick to console me, for he is a veteran of a handful of battles with 20-pound Umpqua steelhead. "You were nothing more than a minor irritation to that fish," Forrest said, "and he never saw reason to get the least bit intimidated."

"That was easily a 20-plus-pound steelhead," Forrest continued and judging by the ten minutes during which we were attached, I've no doubt that I hooked the steelhead of a lifetime that day.

Another winter day on the North Umpqua to be cherished for a lifetime and a reminder during May and June that the river's summer fish are but a month or two away.

Timing The Winter Run

A few winter steelhead often find their way up the North Umpqua by December; still more during January. February through early April, however, offers the bulk of the winter run and consequently provides the best fishing.

These North Umpqua winter steelhead average substantially larger than their summer brethren. Twelve to 15-pound fish are common and a few fish approaching and exceeding 20 pounds are taken each season (most of these by terminal-gear anglers fishing downstream from the fly-only section).

The typical North Umpqua winter run will exceed 6,000 fish, all of them wild North Umpqua stock. Half or less of the winter steelhead will ultimately spawn in the Steamboat/Canton Creek system and as many as 20 percent of the total may end up spawning in tributaries (and in the main river) as far upstream as Soda Springs Dam. Still more fish will use streams below Steamboat, including Rock Creek. Most spawning activity amongst winter steelhead occurs in April and May—several weeks later than the summer steelhead.

By mid-April, one will begin to see steelhead holding on shallow gravel bars in pairs and small groups. These fish are in the act of spawning and etiquette dictates that they be left to their business, undisturbed by anglers.

Winter Steelhead Counts at Winchester Dam, North Umpqua River, 1974-1994

Year	Wild Returns	Hatchery Returns*	Total Returns
1974	7,894	210	8,104
1975	5,744	365	6,109
1976	5,789	223	6,012
1977	5,264	177	5,441
1978	5,949	538	6,487
1979	7,359	452	7,811
1980	7,532	293	7,825
1981	6,580	94	6,674
1982	6,405	**	6,405
1983	3,853	**	3,853
1984	4,588	**	4,588
1985	8,404	**	8,404
1986	10,530	**	10,530
1987	8,153	**	8,153
1988	9,775	**	9,775
1989	7,187	**	7,187
1990	8,537	**	8,537
1991	3,928	**	3,928
1992	5,263	**	5,263
1993	4,366	**	4,366
1994	4,088	**	4,088

*hatchery summer-run steelhead during winter count period
**hatchery summer steelhead in winter count not determined

Winter snow blankets the North Umpqua canyon. Winter steelheaders should be prepared for inclement weather, including snow, anytime between October and April. Joe Howell photo

The swollen flows of winter make many pools unfishable. Still, anglers willing to learn the river will find productive runs during high water periods when few anglers venture to the North Umpqua.

North Umpqua

The North Umpqua's winter fishing subsides as the alders and maples begin to bud on the upper river. Those willing to walk and wade will find on the upper river uncrowded pools whose green-tinted waters hold wild winter steelhead.

Throughout most of the winter season, the North Umpqua will run higher and less clear than during the summer and fall. Still, most winters offer ample opportunity to fish during reasonably low and clear flows. Heavy rains any time during the winter or unusually warm weather that causes massive snow-melt will swell the river rapidly; these heavy flows typically subside in one to three days when more stable conditions return.

Sometimes the river above the Camp Water will run reasonably clear only to have Steamboat Creek discolor the lower section with a glacial-green flow. Even at high water, however, those who know the river well will find places to fish. Joe Howell calls these spots the "high-water holes."

Traditionally, the winter season on the fly-section has gone more-or-less unnoticed by the vast majority of fly anglers. Things are changing now. Each winter greets increasing numbers of anglers bent on trying their luck with the river's wild winter steelhead. Still, a crowded winter day rarely compares to a crowded summer day. Those who fish the winter run often do so under less than perfect conditions. The North Umpqua drainage gets ample precipitation, much of it in the form of rainfall.

Along with the usual cleated boots, a rain parka should be close at hand during a winter-time trip to the North Umpqua.

The same eight- and nine-weight rods that serve so well during the summer are perfectly suited to the winter fishing also. Some kind of sinking-line system will help keep the fly deep in the swollen winter flows. My preference is for a shooting taper system. Usually I opt for a Cortland Type VI sinking "head"

attached to monofilament running line. In the deepest pools I might switch to a heavier head, perhaps a section of 400-grain fly line. A short leader (three to five feet) is well-suited to these fast-sinking heads.

Other anglers might opt for high-density sink-tip fly lines like those designed by Jim Teeny, McKenzie Fly Tackle Company as well as the major line manufacturers. These lines will certainly fish the fly deep, but for me at least, they are more laborious to cast than the head systems.

Many of the North Umpqua's ledge-rock pools are more effectively fished with a weighted pattern. Joe Howell relies on lead-head flies for some of his high-water fishing and he fishes these flies on a ten-foot sink-tip line. With this set-up, he is able to sink a fly quickly in narrow slots where a typical quartering cast proves rather inefficient. Unlike sinking heads, the sink-tip line allows for roll casting, thus opening up just about any kind of water to effective fly fishing.

Those of us who prefer the more traditional flies are confined to certain water types. Luckily, however, the North Umpqua boasts every conceivable kind of water and all of it in abundance.

The patterns used for summer fishing work just as well during the winter, although colored water often begs larger sizes. Some anglers, myself included, often fish Spey-style steelhead patterns during the winter, with the typical shades of orange, black, purple and hot pink being productive. Sizes range from No. 2 to as large as 5/0 and heavy-wire hooks will help keep the fly down during the drift and swing.

Flies Of The North Umpqua

As one would expect, a history of this legendary river would include the origination of numerous patterns dressed specifically for the North Umpqua. Indeed this is the case: Generations of anglers have created numerous North Umpqua dressings, some of which have become standards not only on this river but on steelhead waters everywhere.

I am indebted to Trey Combs—as are we all—for his diligent work in compiling historical data on countless steelhead patterns. His book *Steelhead Fly Fishing and Flies* (Frank Amato Publications, 1976) includes the origins of virtually all the popular steelhead dressings and a great many lesser known ones. Combs' subsequent book, *Steelhead Fly Fishing* (Lyons & Burford, 1991), likewise includes interesting historical information about the origin of many steelhead patterns. Herein I will draw heavily on the work of Combs to highlight the origins of the North Umpqua's best-known flies.

Of all the dressings originated on the North Umpqua, none is more widely recognized than the Skunk, which appeared on the North Umpqua during the 1940s. No doubt a product of several regions, the Skunk is so simple in its design that it would be surprising if only one tier were responsible for its conception. Later, noted photographer Dan Callaghan added the fluorescent green butt, creating the now-popular Green-butt Skunk.

Another widely recognized North Umpqua pattern is the Golden Demon, which Zane Grey brought from New Zealand to southern Oregon in the early 1930s. Not a fly of Northwest origins, the Golden Demon nonetheless remains popular long after Zane Grey's last days fishing the North Umpqua and Rogue Rivers.

Zane Grey's guide Joe DeBernardi (perhaps with Grey's input) may have created the well-known and long-popular Umpqua Special. Exact origins are unknown. Nonetheless, the elegant Umpqua Special remains a popular fly.

Clarence Gordon created a number of flies for his beloved river, the most popular today being the Black Gordon. The Grey Gordon and the Orange Gordon are more-or-less lost to modern steelheading but are still productive and well-conceived dressings.

Gordon and then-Umpqua guide Ward Cummings devised the Cummings or "Cummings Special" during the 1930s. Today it is a steelheading standard, though not so widely known as the Black Gordon.

Other, little-known patterns developed on the North Umpqua include the lovely Stevenson Special, devised by C.N. Stevenson in the 1940s and the Surveyor, essentially a variation on the Umpqua Special that was no doubt named after the Surveyor Hole upstream from Mott Bridge.

Umpqua Special
(tied by the author)

Skunk
(tied by the author)

Cummings Special
(tied by Bob Roberts)

Black Gordon
(tied by Bob Roberts)

Golden Demon
(tied by Bob Roberts)

Jim Schollmeyer

Today, Joe Howell, owner of Blue Heron Fly Shop just across the highway from the river above Idleyld Park, sets the standard for North Umpqua steelhead flies. No doubt several of his creations will be tied by future generations and will take steelhead on the North Umpqua for decades to come.

Joe is especially known for his dry steelhead patterns and for his elegant Spey-style dressings. His Coon Muddler and Flat-head Muddler have become favorites with North Umpqua dry-fly enthusiasts.

Skunk

Tag: Silver
Tail: Red hackle fibers
Body: Black chenille, wool or similar
Rib: Silver tinsel
Throat: Black hackle
Wing: White hair

Umpqua Special

Tail: White hair (bucktail, calftail, polar bear)
Body: Rear third yellow wool, front 2/3 red wool or chenille
Rib: Silver tinsel
Throat: Brown hackle
Wing: White hair with sparse bunches of red hair on either side
Cheeks: Jungle cock

Golden Demon

Tag: Silver or gold tinsel
Tail: Golden pheasant crest
Body: Gold tinsel, embossed or flat with oval or wire rib
Hackle: Orange
Wing: Bronze mallard (according to one source written at the time Zane Grey first visited Oregon's Rogue River) or brown bucktail or similar

Black Gordon

Body: Rear third red wool, front 2/3 black wool or similar
Rib: Gold oval
Throat: Black hackle
Wing: Black bear or similar

Grey Gordon

Tail: Lady amherst tippet
Body: Black dubbing
Rib: Silver tinsel
Throat: Guinea
Wing: Gray squirrel
(dressing as per Combs', *Steelhead Fly Fishing*)

Orange Gordon

Tail: Bronze mallard
Body: Orange wool
Rib: Gold tinsel
Throat: Brown hackle
Wing: Bronze mallard or brown bucktail
(dressing as per Combs', *Steelhead Fly Fishing*)

Cummings Special

Body: Rear third yellow silk or floss, front 2/3 claret wool
Rib: Silver tinsel
Throat: Claret hackle
Wing: Brown bucktail or similar
Cheeks: Jungle cock

Stevenson Special

Tail: Guinea hackle fibers
Body: 3/5 yellow floss, 2/5 black chenille or ostrich
Rib: Gold tinsel
Hackle: Grizzly
Wing: Brown turkey
(dressing as per Combs', *Steelhead Fly Fishing and Flies*)

Surveyor

Tail: Brown over white bucktail
Body: Rear half red tinsel, front half yellow chenille
Rib: Red tinsel through the yellow chenille
Hackle: Grizzly and brown mixed
Wing: White hair with a few strands of red on either side
(dressing as per Combs', *Steelhead Fly Fishing and Flies*)

North Umpqua Spey-style Flies

Thanks in large measure to Joe Howell's creative hand, Spey-style flies have earned a place amongst North Umpqua dressings. The simple, elegant beauty of these flies, with their flowing hackles and low-set wings seem perfectly suited to the resplendent North Umpqua.

Moreover, they catch fish. Large Spey-style dressings, tied on heavy-wire hooks fish beautifully during the higher water of winter; their lightly dressed counterparts offer a delicate profile for skittish summer fish holding in smooth, clear runs and pools.

In recent years, various authors have questioned the usefulness of Spey-style flies in fast water, claiming that the hackles simply collapse under the rigors of rapid currents. Such concerns are a product of contemporary Spey dressings that incorporate any number of different hackles up to and including marabou plumes. Properly constructed, however, these flies fish beautifully in fast flows, namely when the tier adheres to the traditional style of dress: Of the 16 "old Spey flies" listed by A.E. Knox in *Autumns on the Spey* (1872), only three ask for heron hackle. The others call for a cock hackle, taken from the "tail coverts" or in at least one instance, "taken from the neck."

Tied in by the root (or butt) and then spiraled through the body, these cock hackles perform remarkably well even in fast flows. The original Spey flies were tied on a long-shank, light-wire hook with a rather narrow gape. Having experimented with various hooks, I've come to believe that a Dee-style hook such as those used on the original Spey flies helps prevent the fly from swimming sideways or upside down.

For heron-style flies—those tied with long flowing hackle from the rump of a blue-eared pheasant or similar bird—a heavy wire salmon hook, such as the Partridge Code M does a fine job of keeping the fly upright throughout the drift and swing.

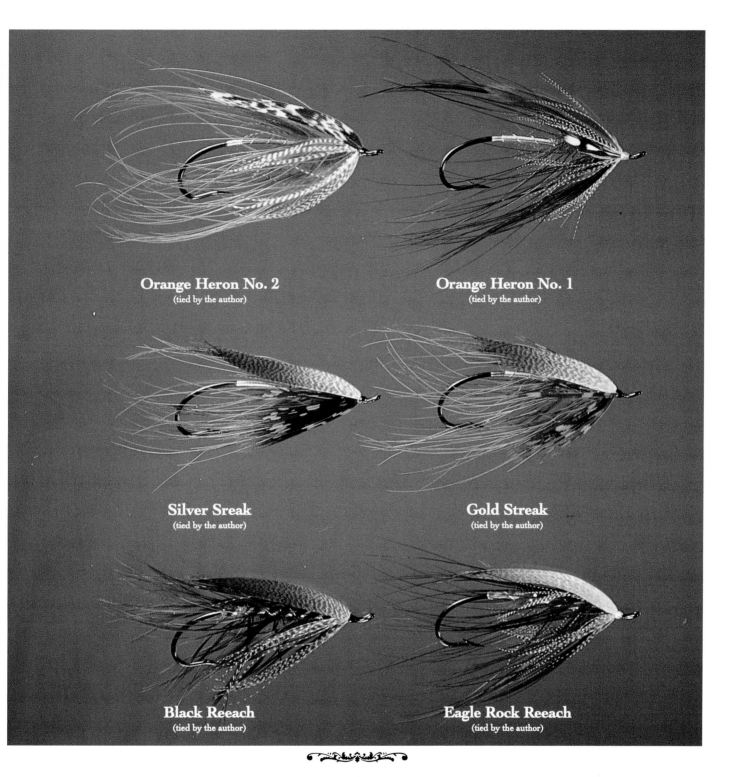

Orange Heron No. 2
(tied by the author)

Orange Heron No. 1
(tied by the author)

Silver Sreak
(tied by the author)

Gold Streak
(tied by the author)

Black Reeach
(tied by the author)

Eagle Rock Reeach
(tied by the author)

Spey-style Dressings
From The North Umpqua

Gold Streak (Joe Howell)

Tag: Flat gold tinsel
Body: Rear half orange floss, front half hot orange seal or
    substitute
Rib: Narrow oval gold
Hackle: Gray heron substitute (e.g. blue-eared pheasant)
Throat: Orange-dyed guinea
Wing: Bronze mallard

Silver Streak (Joe Howell)

Tag: Flat silver tinsel
Body: Flat silver tinsel
Rib: Gold oval
Hackle: Long gray heron substitute (blue-eared pheasant rump)
Throat: Blue-dyed guinea
Wing: Bronze mallard

Orange Heron No. 1 (Joe Howell)

Tag: Flat silver tinsel
Body: Rear half fl. orange floss, front half hot orange seal or similar

Rib: Fine oval gold
Hackle: Black Spey hackle (wide saddle or tail covert), one side stripped, through body
Wing: Four matching fl. orange hackle tips
Throat: Teal
Cheeks: Jungle cock

Orange Heron No. 2 (Joe Howell)

Tag: Flat silver tinsel
Body: Rear half fl. orange floss; front half orange seal or substitute
Rib: Fine gold oval
Hackle: Blue-eared pheasant or similar, through body
Throat: Teal
Wing: Peacock secondary strips

Black Reeach (Shewey)

Body: 1/5 bright orange, 4/5 black seal, angora or fine wool
Hackle: Black cock (tail covert or schlappen) or dyed black blue-eared pheasant rump through body
Ribs: Wide flat gold, narrow flat silver
Counter: Fine gold oval
Throat: Gadwall or teal
Wing: Bronze mallard

Wildflowers, like this trillium, adorn the North Umpqua's banks by mid-spring.

Terry Yamagishi, editor of the Japanese edition of Flyfisherman *magazine, strikes gold. Scott Ripley photo*

Eagle Rock Reeach (Shewey)

Body: 1/5 light orange silk or seal sub., 1/5 hot orange seal or sub., 3/5 deep purple seal or sub.
Hackle: Blue-eared pheasant or similar hackle through body
Ribs: Wide flat gold and narrow flat gold
Counter: Fine silver oval
Throat: Pintail or teal flank
Wing: Bronze mallard

Visitor's Guide To The North Umpqua

If you visit the North Umpqua from out of state, you can fly into Portland or better yet Eugene on the major airlines. Eugene is about two hours from the fly water, Portland, about 4-1/2 hours. From the town of Roseburg, Highway 138 departs Interstate-5 and reaches the North Umpqua at the little community of Glide. From there, the highway parallels the river virtually all the way up the fly water.

From the east side of the Cascade Mountains, Highway 97, the main north-south route in central Oregon, connects with Hwy. 138 about 75 miles south of Bend and about 65 miles north of Klamath Falls. After departing Hwy. 97 at Diamond Lake Junction, Hwy. 138 traverses the Cascades, reaching an elevation of almost 6,000 feet at the top of the pass. This route covers about 30 miles between Diamond Lake Junction and Steamboat.

If you travel this route from central Oregon to the North Umpqua during winter, be prepared for winter storms. I've hit blizzards in late April. The route from Roseburg is more tame, owing to its low elevation. However, Highway 138, especially from Glide eastward, is heavy with log trucks all year and is ripe with narrow, winding curves and nasty potholes. Anglers should strive to keep one eye on the road while the other longs for the river below.

Visitors to the North Umpqua can find lodging ranging from the most rudimentary of fishing camps to the most well-appointed lodging. The latter is available at Steamboat Inn, located just downstream from the famous Camp Water on the highway side of the river.

Steamboat Inn offers cabins at $90 per night, cottages that sleep four and include kitchens at $135 per night and luxurious "honeymoon" suites for two that run $215 per night. The Inn is famous for its meals: The "Fisherman's Dinner" features a full four-course meal—and an excellent one at that—served dining room style to guests seated at monolithic wooden tables.

The dining room speaks volumes of North Umpqua history, with its photographs, framed flies and other paraphernalia. Between eight in the morning and five in the afternoon, Steamboat offers restaurant service as well.

The forest service and the BLM operate campgrounds all along the river. Most open during May, although several (Boulder Flat, Apple Creek, Island, Steamboat Falls, Williams Creek) remain open during the winter. A $5 bill will buy you a night's stay at the campgrounds, but be forewarned: Camp space can be hard to come by on a weekend during the heart of the summer season.

Glide and Idleyld Park, downstream from the lower boundary of the fly water, offer enough services to get you by, including gas, food, drink, some lodging and post offices. Toward the upper end of the fly water, the store at Dry Creek includes a gas pump and a concrete floor that will tolerate your wading spikes if you stop in for a mid-morning or mid-evening cup of coffee.

Guide services can be arranged through Joe Howell at the Blue Heron Fly Shop. While Joe himself no longer guides, he can suggest a competent guide for you.

Blue Heron Fly Shop
HC-60 Box 8-B
Idleyld Park, OR 97447
503-496-0448

Designed by forest service biologists, these log sills below Soda Springs Dam create spawning habitat for steelhead.

The Steamboat Creek drainage is a critical spawning area for the North Umpqua's steelhead.

North Umpqua Campgrounds

Susan Creek Recreation Area (BLM)
Location: On Hwy 138, milepost 29
Campsites: 33
• potable water and flush toilets

Bogus Creek Campground (USFS)
Location: On Hwy 138, milepost 34-35
Campsites: ten improved trailer sites
• five improved tent sites
• potable water and flush toilets

Scaredman Creek Campground (BLM)
Location: On Canton Creek Road off Steamboat Creek Road
Campsites:
• potable water and pit toilets

Island Campground (USFS)
Location: Hwy 138, about a mile upstream from Mott Bridge
Campsites: six improved tent sites
• one improved trailer site
• no potable water; pit toilets

Apple Creek Campground (USFS)
Location: About four miles upstream from Mott Bridge on Hwy. 138

Campsites: six improved tent sites
• two improved trailer sites
• no potable water; pit toilets

Horseshoe Bend Campground (USFS)
Location: Off Hwy 138 above milepost 45, about seven miles upstream from Steamboat
Campsites: 16 improved tent sites
• 18 improved trailer sites
• potable water and flush toilets

Eagle Rock Campground (USFS)
Location: Highway 138 a short distance above Marster's Bridge (appr. milepost 49)
Campsites: 16 improved tent sites
• 8 improved trailer sites
• potable water and pit toilets

Boulder Flat Campground (USFS)
Location: On Highway 138 about three miles upstream from Eagle Rock Campground
Campsites: six improved tent sites
• five improved trailer sites
• potable water and pit toilets

For its entire length the fly water is guarded by tremendous conifers that lean out over the river like sentinals.

The River's Future: Who's Legacy?

"But to make manners on the stream worth-while, there must be some fish in the stream, and the first and greatest obligation of any angler fishing under state ownership is to do nothing that in any way threatens the future of the water he is fishing. This does not mean simply that he must abide by legal restrictions; he must be prepared at times to go beyond this and make regulations for himself. And to make such regulations he needs a certain knowledge of the conditions of the water he is fishing and the essential principles of conservation governing its condition. In other words, he is under at least a moral obligation to understand what makes his sport and why."
—*Roderick Haig-Brown*, The Western Angler, *1947.*

Like so many of our streams, the North Umpqua is a river facing serious threats and has been for decades. While timber harvest and road-building have slackened somewhat in recent years, their effects, along with the effects of the hydro projects on the North Umpqua are reflected in the canyon's ecosystem.

Mark Powell, an aquatic biologist who lives on and studies the North Umpqua, says he finds water quality violations on a daily basis on the North Umpqua during the summer. He is concerned about how the combination of high water temperature and high PH, along with fluctuating temperature and fluctuating PH, affect the river's inhabitants, especially anadromous fish.

Powell, whose research expertise lies in the area of stressful conditions and their effect on aquatic organisms, says that the issue is one of spawning success. He submits that "multiple catch and release, high temperature, which is probably somewhat natural, and high PH, which is very likely not natural, may well be important factors in reproduction success, including egg quality, as well as whether or not eggs are laid."

At the same time, the Oregon Department of Fish and Wildlife continues to release hordes of hatchery summer steelhead into the stream each season, despite the findings of modern science that leave no doubt about the fact that such hatchery operations pose a serious threat to the future of the native fish strains.

Jeff Dose is the head fisheries biologist for the Umpqua National Forest. Prior to his position with the USFS he spent 10 years working for the BLM and a short time working with the Oregon Department of Fish & Wildlife (ODFW). In other words, he's been around the block a time or two and possesses an intimate understanding of the Umpqua basin and the critical issues surrounding its future.

One of his major concerns is that the ODFW hatchery program may pose a severe risk to the river and its native stocks of anadromous fish and he is quick to point out that the "body of scientific literature" leaves little doubt about the negative impact of large-scale hatchery stocks on indigenous fish populations. "We see a tremendous drop-off in productivity when we mix hatchery stock with wild fish," he says.

Unfortunately, as Dose point out, "the forest service and other agencies have no influence on the ODFW hatchery programs." He is concerned over how the ODFW evaluates its programs, saying that "one of my complaints against ODFW is that they fail to evaluate their own projects."

Panther Creek is one of a number of important spawning tributaries to the North Umpqua River.

North Umpqua steelhead are renowned for their long, hard runs.
Joe Howell photo

Powell expresses similar concerns, saying the ODFW's monitoring programs "are pretty superficial."

"My impression," Powell says, "is that there is not a serious questioning attitude (from ODFW) as to whether the hatchery program is beneficial to the system and that questioning attitude should be a key part of any hatchery program in the modern era."

Powell suggests that the ODFW is oriented towards improving the hatchery product to minimize its impact without giving much thought to whether the hatchery stock should be there in the first place.

"I can't say for sure that the (North Umpqua) hatchery program is harmful," Powell continues, "but I think that from everything we know in the research literature, a production hatchery designed to put large numbers of fish in the river and having that superimposed on top of an at least marginally healthy wild population, carries a risk.

Both Powell and Dose agree that the North Umpqua is "refuge habitat." Powell says that "all the modern science suggests that the refuge habitats that are still relatively healthy should be treated as a refuge and not subjected to human impact that carries a risk and the hatchery program I think certainly is not an appropriate treatment for refuge habitat like the North Umpqua should be."

The pattern is classic Northwest fisheries management: For years we dump hatchery fish into a river system in an effort to improve upon Mother Nature only to discover through several decades of scientific study that we are doing more harm than good. For the North Umpqua, the potential, if not actual harm—the risk—continues. The ODFW continues an extensive hatchery program for summer steelhead.

At the same time, the ODFW seems content to pursue a course of what Dose calls "techno-fixes" aimed at improving in-stream habitat to allow for more fish production. The forest service, meanwhile, pursues ecosystem restoration aimed at stabilizing the entire forest ecology. In fact, Dose feels that the ODFW's approach to habitat improvement tends to mask what is really happening.

Powell believes that the ODFW's programs of in-stream habitat improvement would have reaped benefits by now if they were going to succeed in restoring fish populations. He doesn't see that happening. "If that micro-habitat approach were going to restore the fish, they would already be back and that includes trout."

"We have a salmon and trout crisis, not just a salmon crisis," notes Powell. "Trout should be doing better unless freshwater habitat was a critical problem."

Powell notes that if ocean conditions were to blame for our shrinking runs of anadromous runs, then wild trout would claim the niche voided by shrinking populations of salmon and steelhead smolt. Yet this is not the case. He says that the in-stream, in-channel work pursued by ODFW "is about the most extreme example of ineffective band-aid mitigation that I've ever seen."

Dave Loomis, the district biologist for the ODFW in Roseburg, says that the forest service doesn't support the kind of micro-habitat, in-channel work performed by the ODFW. "They call it a band-aid approach," complains Loomis. He says the forest service is more concerned with things like road stabilization and the health of the watershed in general. "We don't disagree with that approach," says Loomis, but he points out that the ODFW sees in-stream improvement as an important factor in stabilizing the health of the watershed by providing good spawning habitat for salmon and steelhead.

Perhaps the ODFW cannot be held too much at fault for its inclination towards in-stream, micro-habitat improvements: After all, the ODFW's basic historical purpose is to oversee fishing and hunting in the state of Oregon, not necessarily to see to the health of our forest ecosystems in general. Moreover, lots of ODFW jobs depend upon and exist because of the hatchery program. Still, ecological science has demonstrated for years that you cannot change one part of the ecosystem without affecting the other parts.

Powell says that the ODFW does not regularly participate in scientific conferences where the latest findings and methods are discussed by a wide spectrum of individuals. Dose agrees, saying, "my own personal observation is that the (ODFW district) people are not participants in the science, they don't contribute to the science, they don't read the literature apparently. I never see them at conventions and workshops and symposiums. They don't publish anything; they are not really involved in the science per se.

"I think ODFW has some tremendous research biologists who have contributed vitally to the science of ecosystem restoration," Dose continues, "but they (ODFW) have the other side that has a lot more decision-making authority."

Both Powell and Dose, along with other people interested in protecting the North Umpqua, express concern about a Roseburg-based group called the Umpqua Basin Fisheries

Scott Ripley

Restoration Initiative. According to Powell, this group has failed to meet the state standards that would allow it to become a watershed council, "primarily because the Umpqua Basin Group and the Douglas County Commissioners reject the notion of scientific and technical oversight."

The group, Powell says, "is not interested in an honest and open discussion of all issues and that is the reason this group has been rejected as an official state-chartered watershed council even though many other biased and unbalanced groups have successfully been chartered. This group is so far out there versus state standards that they can't get chartered.

"The problem that I have with the group," Powell continues, "is that it is pretty much an unbalanced membership. It is tilted pretty heavily toward resource-using agencies and industries and leans pretty heavy away from what you might call conservation groups and individuals."

Dose has made presentations to the Initiative and sat in on a few meetings.

"They claim to be facilitators not decision makers," he says. Dose points out, however, that "a lot of what transpires after those meetings is ineffective in terms of restoring ecosystem functions. That's been just in my observation."

The Initiative does, in fact, exert some influence over lands administered by the federal government (forest service and BLM). Dose points to a recent "watershed restoration" project on Canton Creek, an important spawning area and a major tributary to Steamboat Creek. "There was kind of a joint BLM-forest service restoration program that was conducted up there in 1994," explains Dose. "It was an outgrowth of watershed analysis that was required under the president's plan.

"What was recommended by forest service biologists was primarily inventory to get a better understanding of watershed processes and functions so that effective restoration could be done," Dose continues. "That didn't happen," he says, "Instead there was a bunch of road reconstruction, paving, chip sealing, bridge repair, and a few in-stream structures were constructed and none of those things were really considered high priority and some were considered not even appropriate by forest service fisheries biologists . . .so they did have quite an influence there, at least in 1994.

"They (the Initiative) basically overruled and didn't follow the recommendations made by experienced forest service fisheries biologists," Dose says.

North Umpqua brown trout.

Despite the North Umpqua's popularity and rich history, many small runs remain little known and virtually unfished.

Dose points out, however, that the group seems to have a lot more influence with the BLM than with the forest service. "I think the BLM is a very avid supporter and real active in the group and in some ways have kind of abrogated their own fisheries responsibilities," he continues.

"Those are my personal opinions as an interested professional fisheries biologist, but probably not the official line of the agency," Dose cautions. "I am not empowered to speak for the agency."

Powell points out that the forest service, by participating in the group, "is in essence endorsing at some level what is going on despite the fact that many individuals in the agency have some real problems with the way things are proceeding."

Both Powell and Dose, along with other interested parties, agree that, as Powell puts it, "certainly the forest service resource professionals and even the forest service activities are by far the most scientifically credible efforts in the Umpqua Basin. The BLM is a distant second and the ODFW is not even in the ball park.

"The forest service is, in my opinion, the most progressive element in the area," Powell says.

"That is not to say that every person in the forest service is progressive," he continues, "but the forest service employs the most up-to-date and credible fisheries scientists of any one in the Umpqua Basin."

Joe Howell, critical about certain forest service activities, praises Jeff Dose as an outspoken critic of some of his agency's own policies in resource management. Of the forest service, Dose says simply, "we can do better."

The good news, according to Dose, is that much of the forest ecosystem itself is essentially on the rebound after decades of heavy timber harvest. Timber is no longer harvested from

Steamboat Creek, allowing the drainage to stabilize. "We have ceased doing many of the things that we used to do, the things that caused much of the harm," says Dose.

Dose says that there is a lot left to save in the North Umpqua drainage. After all, the North Umpqua boasts six strains of indigenous anadromous fish, although passage of searun cutthroat over Winchester Dam has all but ceased.

Still, Dose warns that "there is a lot of green gold left in those hills." He cautions further that representatives and interested parties from timber-related industries, as a public, make themselves heard more loudly than anyone else. Dose suggests that anglers concerned about the North Umpqua's future should do likewise, making their concerns known and voicing their opinions to federal and state agencies as well as politicians and bureaucrats.

Powell agrees that we should make our views known. Powell says it is "important to get involved and support the efforts of local groups like the Steamboaters."

One of his main concerns lies in trying to ensure that the critical issues surrounding the North Umpqua are openly discussed and are on the table. Like Dose, he is concerned that forest management in the Umpqua National Forest along with the hydro projects, which are up for re-licensing in 1997, stick to the letter and intent of the new forest plan and the Wild and Scenic Rivers plan. Both Powell and Dose suggest that now more than ever the fly fishing community should make itself heard.

Joe Howell, likewise, suggests that anglers write letters to state and federal agencies. In dealing with these agencies, he suggests letters to the regional and local offices as well as the Portland offices.

Meanwhile, as we fight the traditional battles over ecosystem protection and recovery, new threats are emerging. Chief among these is the rapid increase of recreational use on the North Umpqua, much of this in the form of boat traffic. Rafters and kayakers are an increasingly common sight. More than just a nuisance to anglers, the boaters threaten spawning steelhead and salmon by pushing the fish off their redds.

Anglers too are at fault for disturbing spawning fish. In most cases I would argue that some anglers simply don't care that they are casting to fish on redds. In other instances, perhaps the guilty party simply doesn't know the difference between spawning fish and holding fish.

To many if not most West-coast steelhead fly anglers, pursuing fish on the redds is the moral equivalent of snagging. Unfortunately, not all fly anglers feel that way and because of that, area and/or time closures may be a forthcoming part of the body of regulations concerning the North Umpqua's fly-only section.

In any event, the future seems unclear for the North Umpqua, but certainly the river has a chance. Jeff Dose says "clearly if you look at the number of remaining fairly pure stocks of fish that are still there, if you look at the relative health of the aquatic system, particularly the mainstem—I think that anyone would look at that and say this is a pretty unique place relative to everywhere else in this state. It definitely is a refuge area and should require extra special protection. I believe that you can't restore unless you protect first. I think it is possible to protect and not restore and be somewhat successful over time but to try to restore without protecting is absurd."

Scott Ripley

North Umpqua

The Steamboaters

The Steamboaters have been an integral force in preserving the fly fishing legacy of the North Umpqua. Membership is open to anyone, but on a sponsorship basis (a current member must sign your membership application as your sponsor). Joe Howell has sponsored many new members over the years. You can call Joe for information or contact the Steamboaters at the address listed below.

The membership of about 300 is widespread, representing many states as well as other nations. The purpose and mission of the Steamboaters "shall be to preserve, promote, and restore the natural production of wild fish populations, especially steelhead, the habitat which sustains them, and the unique aesthetic values of the North Umpqua River for present and future generations."

Steamboaters
P.O. Box 7066
Eugene, OR 97401

A Social Question?

Frank Moore is sickened by what he sees these days on the North Umpqua: fly anglers, standing in one place for hours, drifting weighted nymphs under huge strike indicators. Joe Howell wanted to escape for a day last winter so he headed upstream for the Camp Water, which was occupied by two anglers already. He drove on past, fished upriver for four hours and returned to the Camp Water only to find the same two anglers still standing in their respective places. No chance for Joe to fish through those magical runs on his beloved river.

The North Umpqua offers something for everyone. Those who enjoy long casts and deep wades through classic steelhead pools will find abundant possibilities.

Joe Howell with a North Umpqua hatchery steelhead.

The nymph/indicator anglers have stirred a controversy on the North Umpqua: Most of them stand in one place, clogging up the runs in total defiance of traditional steelheading etiquette, casting heavily weighted flies with large globs of yarn for indicators. Their tackle defines their method more as drift-fishing than as fly fishing, or as my friend Forrest Maxwell says, "they are drift-fishing with fly rods."

Forrest goes on to suggest that they could fish far more effectively if they would attach their weighted nymph/indicator system to a light-weight drift rod."

Frank Moore, Joe Howell and many other North Umpqua anglers would like to see this method regulated off the river for a simple reason: The method is effective to the point that it defies the original intent of the fly-only regulation. "How many times can a steelhead be hooked and fought before its energy reserves are depleted to the point that it cannot spawn?" asks Joe Howell. His concerns are echoed by Frank Moore.

Dave Loomis, Jim Van Loan (state game commissioner and owner of Steamboat Inn) and Jerry Bauer (one-time fisheries biologist for the Umpqua district) all more-or-less agree that this is a "social issue" that probably should not be solved through the regulatory process. Certainly their point is well taken: After all, the fly angling fraternity can be its own best friend by trying to educate and inform its members. What we cannot do, I contend, is change attitudes.

My training in public relations taught me some valuable lessons, among them the idea that you are generally wasting time and resources when you attempt to change an attitude. Through education we can perhaps alter opinions and thus change behavior, but we cannot easily change attitudes.

Joe Howell calls it a "numbers game," this practice of nymph-and-indicator fishing for steelhead on the North Umpqua. Myself and many others concur. During my years working in fly shops I encountered many folks—and exponentially more from the early 1980s onward—who saw fly fishing as a competitive endeavor, where catching lots of fish was to win and and not catching lots of fish was to lose. In other words, the ends justify and far outweigh the means. Lost on these people is the idea that fly fishing is an art and as such a spiritual endeavor.

This idea that fly fishing is a competitive endeavor—a zero-sum game if you will—is an attitude. It is a deeply held belief that is not easily changed; it is part of the fabric of one's psyche. In some anglers, these attitudes will change over time: I remember still my first days fishing as a child. At the age of nine I was loose in the backwoods of Idaho, chasing cutthroat on beaver-dammed streams. My overriding goal and desire was to catch fish. As my years on-stream accumulated, I digressed from a kid who simply loved to catch fish to an angler who took pride in catching more and bigger fish. In my late teens I began to realize that the fishing itself was more important to me than the catching. This was a critical evolution in my attitudes and one that many outdoorsmen go through.

Of nouveau fly anglers—and this includes many of the indicator fishermen on the North Umpqua—I believe this transition has not yet been realized. They have not yet learned of the art in fly fishing. They have not yet realized that the means itself justifies the ends, not the other way around. They have not yet realized that the joy of fishing this splendid river is privilege enough and that to bring a steelhead to the fly is a reward most cherished when done in a gentlemanly manner. It is my hope that many such fishermen will eventually experience the evolution in attitude that allows them to understand how valuable is this experience of fly fishing for steelhead. Some never will.

So do we wait for attitudes to change and at the same time use education to help form and shape opinions? By all means yes and in saying that I certainly agree that, in some ways, this is a social issue. But cannot a social issue be solved in part through the regulatory process?

I am an avid bird hunter. Market hunting of waterfowl and other fowl drove certain species into extinction around the turn of the century. This was a social issue: Do we allow market hunting to continue until populations are decimated or do we use the regulatory process to curb the tide? We did the latter. Sport hunting harvest is huge. We use the regulatory process to set limits on our kill. Sportsmen abide by the limits. Toxic shot was said to be a problem. We changed to non-toxic varieties when rules said we must. We waterfowlers have tolerated—and supported—countless and increasing restrictions: Ever narrowing bag limits and complicated species restrictions, severe limits on the hours we can hunt, restrictions on shot sizes, limits on the number of shells allowed in the gun and in some places even a limit on the numbers of shells allowed in possession. In the name of maintaining a tradition, waterfowlers abide by the ever-tightening noose around our collective necks.

Most of these regulations force a change in our behavior without changing basic attitudes. The waterfowler believes deeply in a fundamental right to hunt ducks and geese.

Hence I find repugnant this idea that a so-called social issue cannot in part be solved through the regulatory process. Perhaps the issue is more one of defining the problem or more specifically, defining nymph/indicator fishing on the North Umpqua as a problem.

Before we can tackle that issue, we must first understand the complexities of nymph-indicator fishing: As per my discourse above, it should be quite apparent that this method is nothing more than drift fishing with a fly rod and differs from the classic method of fly fishing for steelhead in a critical and defining way: With the classic steelheading methods we are trying to motivate the steelhead to leave the comfort of his rest and chase the fly. The practitioner of the indicator/nymph method does the oppo-

Forrest Maxwell shoots line across a favorite pool below Marster's Bridge on the upper river.

The North Umpqua boasts a population of indigenous cutthroat trout, including the sea-run variety. In recent years, however, the sea-run cutthroat of the North Umpqua have virtually disappeared. With these "bluebacks" essentially gone and the North Umpqua's coho salmon severely reduced, what can we surmise about the future of the river's native steelhead and Chinook salmon? Anglers and biologists alike are searching for such answers.

site. He attempts to drift the fly directly into the steelhead's lair, the closer the better. The difference is monumental: The classic steelheader attempts to bring a fish to the fly; the nympher attempts to bring a fly to the fish. This is no subtle difference.

If you are riding the fence on this issue, perhaps leaning one direction or the other, I urge you to consider this carefully: If the goal is to drift a weighted lure as close to the steelhead as possible, then how does this method differ from traditional drift-fishing with a spinner, spoon, corkie, wobbler or glob of bait? In my estimation, the only difference is in the kind of rod, reel and line employed and as such I would agree with Forrest Maxwell that the indicator/nympher would be even more effective if he were to attach his weighted fly to a light-weight level-wind outfit.

Now let's examine our North Umpqua history. Dave Loomis supplied me with a brief outline of the history of the decision to create the fly-only water on the North Umpqua. Loomis writes that "the use of wobblers, flatfish, flashers and spinners, in combination with the newly available spinning gear, caused the continued hooking of adult salmon and steelhead. Mr. Pitney was quoted as explaining the results of a recent study as 'even though they may not kill the fish, the same fish may be hooked and played to exhaustion several times until it becomes weakened, dying before spawning season as a result.'"

This quote from then-biologist William E. Pitney came in 1951, the year that he and district game supervisor James Vaughn submitted to the Game Commission the initial regulation proposal to establish the fly-only water. Loomis says they were "cited as saying the reason for needing this proposal was 'to halt heavy losses of undersized trout, salmon, and steelhead, while at the same time, providing greater measure of protection for adult salmon and summer steelhead.'"

One of the overriding questions posed by myself and many others is thus: If the original intent of establishing the fly-only water was to increase protection for adult salmon and summer steelhead by assuring that they were no longer subject to increasingly productive drift- and spin-fishing methods, then why do we allow drift-fishing with a fly rod to continue on the fly water and on the Camp Water in particular?

I posed that question to Loomis. "It's a good point," he said. "When have we gotten to a point where the indicator fishermen pose a biological concern?

"If it does get to be a biological concern, I am likely to suggest that we limit the take by looking at seasonal closures or area closures. We want the opportunity for fly fishing with a variety of methods to continue."

Loomis insists that the department does not want social issues to stand in the way of biological decisions. To that end, ODFW policy will be aimed at recommending regulations that emanate from a biological need. Loomis points out that anglers will always find ways to legally circumvent regulations and that continually upgrading and changing regulations to compensate for changes in technique and tackle is policy that is not based on biology.

No doubt he is correct that changes in regulations (concerning methods and tackle) aimed at reducing the effectiveness of angling to afford a level of protection to the fish would be at least somewhat temporary in nature since anglers would soon devise ways to legally circumvent certain tackle restrictions. Indeed, the history of the North Umpqua is one ripe with temporary, transitory regulations.

Still, I find it difficult to escape the fact that the North Umpqua's fly-only restriction was originally devised as a method of offering some safe harbor to salmon and steelhead. Given that intent, it seems that indicator-nymph fishing would fall under the category of methods that, by its intent, the proposal intended to eliminate from a section of the river. Obviously, the indicator method was not in use during the 1940s and '50s, but I believe it would have been seen as inappropriate for the fly water because of its inherent similarity—both in method and in results—to the kinds of techniques that were, by the establishment of the fly-only section, outlawed for the protection of the fish.

Frank Moore says in no uncertain terms that this method of fishing "is exactly the kind of thing we sought to eliminate by creating the fly-only section."

Moore served on the commission from 1969-74 and before that was deeply involved with the establishment of the fly-only section in the early 1950s. He doesn't buy the argument that the indicator issue is a social one. "It's not a social issue, it's a protective issue," he says.

If indeed the intent of the law was to reduce the effectiveness of sport fishing for the protection of salmon and steelhead above Rock Creek, then Frank Moore and Joe Howell and all the rest of us who fall into the same camp must be correct in defining this issue as a protective one and moreover we must be correct in defining the indicator/weighted nymph method as the kind of technique that the original restrictions sought to banish from a certain section of the river.

Certainly anyone can appreciate the need to allow sound biological reasoning to dictate policy regarding sport fishing and harvest. But as Frank Moore so vividly points out, this is precisely the reason why we should remove the weighted nymph/indicator technique from the fly-only water: For the protection of the fish.

The kind of restriction that would reduce the effectiveness of this deadly form of angling is quite simple: Change the law to allow for a single, unweighted fly and no additional attachments to the leader. But here is where we encounter the snag. The North Umpqua is a fly-only river, but not a fly fishing-only river. The distinction is critical. So long as they use a fly, anglers are allowed to fish with a spinning or casting outfit, thus allowing for the use of casting bubbles and flies. The regulation in 1995 read as follows:

"Restricted to the use of a single artificial fly, any type of rod or reel permitted but with no metal core lines and no added weights or attachments except a floating bubble or similar floating device."

How can we tell fly anglers they cannot use indicators while spin fishermen are allowed to use casting bubbles? The answer is an obvious one: Make the North Umpqua a fly fishing-only river by restricting anglers to fly rod, fly reel and fly line. Such a regulation change occurred in 1980, but the commission yielded to public outcry from the terminal-tackle community and the restriction was lifted within months.

Dave Loomis says that the "North Umpqua always receives the biggest pile of proposals for regulation changes."

I suggest the ODFW and the commission receive a lot more proposals aimed at making this fly-only river into a fly fishing-only river. Only then can we address the methodology employed by our own by pushing for a regulation eliminating additional attachments to the leader while simultaneously trying to teach the

Spawning steelhead in the North Umpqua. While summer steelhead primarily spawn in tributary streams, many winter fish spawn in the main river channel. Anglers should recognize these spawning steelhead and leave them alone.

Fawn lilies (Erythronium) *blooming along the river banks near Boulder Flat.*

After all, no other method allows you to become so intimate with the river and no other technique brings out so much in the steelhead.

Imagine wading into the top of a steelhead run, intent on fishing through, only to have an angler step into the tailout without first asking? The only thing that could make matters worse would be to have that angler stand in one spot, ruining your opportunity to fish out the pool. Similarly, imagine walking the trail to a favorite run only to find an angler already standing in the middle of the pool. You sit on a rock to wait your turn, but soon you realize the other fellow is not moving. Steelhead fly fishing etiquette be damned.

Nymphers certainly aren't the only ones guilty of ignoring steelheading etiquette: I've had the same thing happen while waiting to fish behind traditional anglers. They spot a fish holding in a pool and stand there for an hour more, changing flies over and over in an attempt to rise the fish. Certainly a sighted fish deserves some extra time and effort, but if a strike is not forthcoming after what seems an appropriate amount of time, others waiting behind should be allowed to fish through.

Unfortunately, part of the nymph-indicator technique involves repeated casts and drifts through the same area—many more so to a sighted fish. I won't argue that a well-seasoned practitioner of this method can cover a fair amount of water without clogging up a particular run for too long, but what of the more numerous anglers who use the technique with less practice and skill?

They find a visible fish and then subject that fish with drift after drift until one presentation essentially leads the fly into the steelhead's jaws. Meanwhile they stand in one place for an inordinate amount of time. No need to hone distance-casting skills nor perfect those elegant long-line mends because the nymph-indicator angler needn't be concerned with covering large pools with the classic taut-line swing. In short, this technique requires less of an investment in skill and practice per number of fish hooked.

But as Clark C. Van Fleet wrote, "It does not require much more effort to be skillful—and it is a real part of the enjoyment."

This age of increasing pressures on our outdoor resources dictates more than ever that fly anglers recognize and practice time-

virtues of classic steelheading to new inductees to the sport. Of all the people I spoke with while compiling this project, not a single one questioned the intent of the original fly-only law: To make sport fishing less effective on salmon, steelhead and smolts.

Perhaps then, we fly anglers who wish to see the North Umpqua retain its inherent grace, should increase the pressure on the ODFW and the commission to deal effectively with this controversial body of regulations. To this point, the commission and the ODFW seem to be continually intimidated by pressure from local people who express the grand old concern over losing their rights to fish as their father and grandfather did. That is an attitude we can't hope to change. What we may be able to do, however, is demonstrate our own resolve by adding substantially to that "pile of proposals" concerning the North Umpqua.

Oregon Fish and Wildlife Commission
P.O. Box 59
Portland, OR 97207

Oregon Department of Fish & Wildlife
P.O. Box 59
Portland, OR 97207

A Question Of Etiquette

All that said, it seems absurd to me that the fly angling community should even need to deal with this situation. "Given the chance," I ask myself, "why would anyone choose not to employ the traditional method of taking steelhead on a down-and-across presentation?"

Biologists counting smolts.

Richard T. Grost

North Umpqua

Forrest Maxwell filets a hatchery steelhead at he and the author's "steelhead camp" at Eagle Rock Campground.

honored and time-tested river etiquette. Foremost among steelhead fly fishing rules of behavior is the importance of moving through a pool. I am reminded of the old writers, who sought to educate their readers on the importance of etiquette and on the importance of pursuing their art in a gentlemanly manner (no sexism intended). Today's body of contemporary literature seeks to inform. Give them the information they need to catch fish and you will sell articles and sell books. Try to spin a yarn and weave a tale and offer ideas of sportsmanship: the magazines see it as too wordy. The goal of the majority of today's writing is to tell anglers how to catch more and bigger fish; it is the rare piece that tells them how to do so in a gentlemanly manner.

From Roderick Haig-Brown, in *The Western Angler:*

> It is not altogether easy to lay down a set of rules on "how to behave while fishing a public water"; so much depends on the temperament of the individual. But it is safe enough to say to all but the very meek, "Over do the good manners." The main thing is to give the other fellow plenty of room; if he is fishing down a pool ahead of you, don't crowd him from behind. If you cut in below him, cut in well below—a hundred or two hundred yards, if possible, not just fifty or a hundred feet. As a general rule, don't cut in below him; let him work well down, then start in behind him and be content to stay there. It's easy enough to pick up a fish behind a good fisherman, because he won't disturb the ones he doesn't get, and generally it is just as easy to pick them up behind a clumsy fisherman, because he leaves them all there for you. And if you are fishing down ahead and someone behind seems impatient—let him go on through. You'll take your time and cover the water better if you do.

And from Claude Krieder in *Steelhead*, 1948:

> Sporting ethics entail consideration of other anglers in these days of heavily fished waters, and there is a certain code that properly applies where many anglers gather on a popular pool or riffle. The casters should start toward the head of the water and work through in turn, each angler following the next and a decent interval behind. Thus each has an opportunity to test his skills the entire length of the pool, and no man may appropriate any one spot as his own without soon learning by hint—or plain forcible language—that he is not playing the game.

Indeed, those very concepts in steelheading etiquette are spelled out on a sign at the parking area above the Camp Water near Mott Bridge. Yet they are ignored by a small but highly visible minority who seem to prefer hooking lots of fish by whatever means necessary than to hook a few fish in a gentlemanly manner. As I've told people before, shooting ducks on the water is awfully damn effective, but that doesn't make it sporting and the shooter who does so is liable to hear an earful from other hunters.

Perhaps fly anglers need to act a little more like duck hunters: Let our feelings be heard on the stream when it comes to issues concerning the ethics and etiquette of our sport.

To be sure there are steelheaders on the North Umpqua who fish the traditional tackle and technique but ignore traditional etiquette: They don't move through a pool; they step in immediately below another angler; they don't ask before entering an occupied pool. They are as much or more of a problem as the nymphers who stand in one place for hours.

On most any other river I would not object to an angler drift-fishing with a fly rod so long as he or she did so while adhering to steelheading etiquette when another angler wishes to fish through the pool. But on the North Umpqua this question is not merely one of etiquette: It is foremost a question of affording some measure of protection to steelhead that are highly visible in super-clear water and highly confined in ledge-bound runs.

Those of us who profess to practice traditional steelheading etiquette can be our own best friends by going out of our way to promote the classic steelheading techniques and their inherent set of codes. Indeed, I would suggest that we are under something of an obligation to do so—a view that I think will hold increasingly more merit as the number of anglers increases on the North Umpqua and our other beloved Northwest steelhead rivers.

Chinook salmon spawning below Marster's Bridge on the upper river. Traditionally, the North Umpqua received tremendous runs of both Chinook and coho salmon. Today their numbers are much reduced.